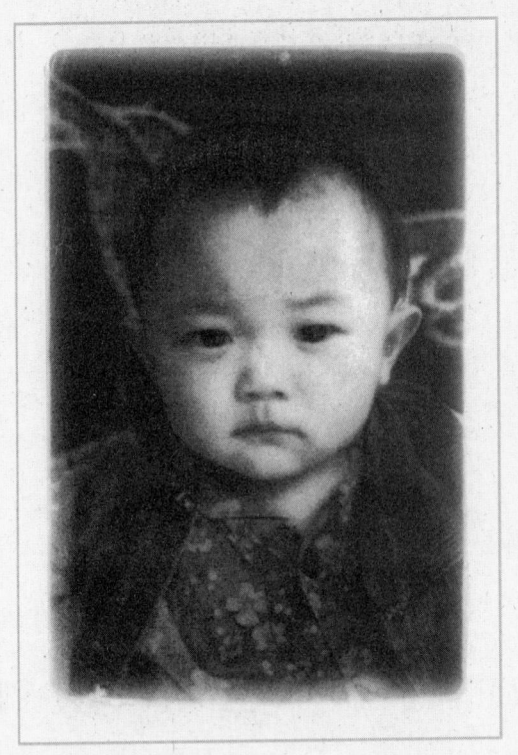

An Unexpected Mother's
Journey to Adoption in China

Forever Lily

BETH NONTE RUSSELL

A TOUCHSTONE BOOK
PUBLISHED BY SIMON & SCHUSTER
New York   London   Toronto   Sydney

Touchstone
Rockefeller Center
1230 Avenue of the Americas
New York, NY 10020

Copyright © 2004, 2007 by Beth Nonte Russell
All rights reserved,
including the right of reproduction
in whole or in part in any form.

TOUCHSTONE and colophon are registered trademarks of Simon & Schuster, Inc.

"Lament" copyright © 1982 by Stephen Mitchell, from *The Selected Poetry of Rainer Maria Rilke* by Rainer Maria Rilke, translated by Stephen Mitchell. Used by permission of Random House, Inc.

For information regarding special discounts for bulk purchases,
please contact Simon & Schuster Special Sales at 1-800-456-6798 or
business@simonandschuster.com.

Designed by Jan Pisciotta

Manufactured in the United States of America

10   9   8   7   6   5   4   3

Library of Congress Cataloging-in-Publication Data is available.

ISBN-13: 978-0-7432-9297-9
ISBN-10:   0-7432-9297-9

For those left behind

Forever Lily

Prologue

Hanging suspended above the world, on a terrace overlooking the steely waters of the harbor below, I watch as boats glide by in uncanny silence. All seems in its proper place, a projection of my own inner calm thrown onto the screen of the world.

Twilight, and the light is fading. A thick, opalescent mist shrouds the skyline, and the buildings in the distance blink on and off, sometimes visible, sometimes disappearing behind a shimmering veil. Tomorrow it will be a memory, as yesterday it was a dream. Is any of this real, are any of us?

I am not sure anymore. One night a year ago, I was alone, staying in a house I had rented for a month at the beach. On the last night, I woke with the feeling that I had just been falling, spiraling through a dark abyss. The first thing I noticed was the silence in the room, pressing in on me like something tangible, my senses heightened and on full alert. What was that? I felt certain that someone had been speaking. And then, I was sure; a voice . . . I heard a voice.

A distinctive voice, arising in my mind, somewhat like a memory, but completely new and unknown to me, a part of me and yet separate. I could hear the voice, and though at first the words were unintelligible, they became more and more clear. I scrambled to find my pen and my journal, and began to write the words that were streaming through my head:

How is it possible to be reborn if you do not die? It is my most urgent wish to be reborn. It is the only wish I have now, the only desire left to me. Everything else, all passion, all hope, slowly fades to the point where I cannot see it anymore. It is difficult for me to even imagine a time when passion moved me, or hope lifted me. I want nothing that I used to want, which makes me not the person that I used to be. We create ourselves through what we desire, and I don't know who I am anymore.

Dying is nothing like we suppose. It is an unshackling, a freedom I never knew in life. Strangely, I am not less myself, but more. And those things I am losing as life ebbs from my body are the very things that kept me enslaved. The fears and desires, all the time mistaken for my real self, now recede into unreality. They are dying, not I, not I. . . .

In this state between life and death I can see both where I am going and where I have been. It is this realization of continuity that allows me to release myself from this earth, from the loves I have known here. For when fear and desire die, only the unspeakable reality of love remains. My daughter, my Little Bird . . . my love will follow you through time until you too break free from this existence, triumphant. I see you laughing into the wind as you run, knowing that the sun that warms you is me, and the song of the birds is me, and the deep longing you have is me also. We are one, and in this oneness we will be together forever.

You will live, and as I spiral upward into the next phase of my existence, I use all my strength to hold the thought of you, to pull the essence of this love into the center of my heart, where it will remain a dormant seed of joy until we meet again. My wish now is to be reborn, a most urgent wish, and the only true longing I have ever known.

"Dying is nothing like we suppose . . ."? I put down my pen and stared at the words that had just been written. A part of me had just stepped aside, a space had been made, and something else . . . someone else . . . had come pouring through the opening, and out onto the page. A voice, familiar and yet unknown to me, had emerged full-blown into my consciousness, expressing a love and longing beyond my known experience. What did this mean, what did this mean about who I am?

"My daughter, my Little Bird . . ."; those poignant words could not have come from me, for I had no daughter to speak to or long for. The intensity of the longing expressed made me ask myself for what, for whom, would I die in order to be reborn? Something had been winding down in me for a long time and that is why I went there, to the rented house near the sea, to decide about my life.

Standing here a year later, on the other side of the world, I realize that I have been waiting for that golden moment the voice had whispered of, the moment when fear and desire die, and only the unspeakable reality of love remains.

Time

When I wake, I don't know where I am. It takes several minutes before I remember I am on my way to China, I am traveling with my friend Alex, we are going to bring home a baby. The sun is still shining, though according to my watch it is ten o'clock in the evening. We have been following the light since this morning as we have flown over the top of the world, and it has been eerie, a day with no night. We could be anywhere, it could be any time, in this moment, suspended between heaven and earth; I am flying into tomorrow, or is it yesterday?

There are still several hours before we are scheduled to land in Tokyo, and from there, we will take a three-hour flight to Beijing. I have an entire row to myself; this airplane is almost empty. Several books, all of which I am having trouble concentrating on, surround me on the seat, and the remains of a half-eaten lunch still wait to be taken away by the flight attendant. I look across the aisle and see that Alex is stretched out, sleeping. After more than a year of planning for this adoption, it must finally be starting to seem real for her; she seems distracted, withdrawn, and not in the mood to chat about the new baby or anything else.

I have spent the time on the plane trying to read, looking out at the clouds, thinking—the things I prefer to do anyway. At some point I began to meditate, but I must have fallen asleep; there was a dream, something intense . . . what was it? I try hard to bring it back; I recall a structure, bathed in dreamlight, and as I concentrate on this image, more details begin to emerge from the shadows of sleep. I take out my notebook and pen to record what I remember:

I am standing near a pagoda, surrounded by water. I am looking at my reflection, when suddenly another reflection merges with mine. I look up to see a young Chinese man, in some type of military or royal dress. He is standing behind me. My heart rises up in joy and yet I am also afraid. I can see that I am dressed in some type of elegant robe, with elaborate embroidery and color. The man does not speak and neither do I, but we seem to understand each other without words. Somehow, I know that he loves me, and I feel my love for him rise in return. We melt together in a swirl of energy that is unlike anything I have felt before. When we finally separate, we walk together to look into the water, and see a lotus flower that is vibrating and throwing off light. In the dream I know that this flower symbolizes pure love.

The dream is a shimmering little jewel, so vivid in color and feeling. I have had so many dreams about China since I agreed to come on this trip with Alex: dreams about babies, dreams that I am Chinese and that Alex is Chinese, and a dream in which Alex's husband is a Chinese soldier trying to warn me of some danger. There have been so many dreams, in fact, that I mentioned them to Alex, in mid-October, six weeks before we were to travel to China. I am thinking of telling her about this one, too, when I hear the captain announce that we are preparing to descend. Alex joins me in my row, and we begin to gather our belongings. She is still quiet and withdrawn, her face white and tired-looking. A tiny twinge of homesickness rises in me, and there are butterflies in my stomach. It already feels as if we've been gone for a lifetime.

This morning when we met at the airport, it was cold and dark, a crystal clear December morning; our husbands and

Alex's son were there to see us off. Alex lingered with them while I stood off to the side with my luggage. This was a big moment for their family, a turning point, an ending and a beginning. No longer would it be just the three of them; a new baby would join them and change their lives. I could tell they were unsure about this, hesitant, not smiling, clinging to one another. I thought of the little face in the picture Alex had shown me a few weeks ago, a black-eyed girl with sparse hair and a determined look. The orphanage had sent the picture of the baby assigned to her, and when Alex showed it to me, I asked for a copy of the photo, and then pasted it onto the front cover of the journal I would be keeping for this trip.

Writing during my travels has become a habit for me. Somehow, a trip feels incomplete if I do not end it with a set of pages recorded during the journey. So much is lost, so much not even noticed, unless it is thought about, contemplated, and integrated during the writing process. There is a shelf of travel journals in my bookcase at home, evidence that I have been somewhere, and that I have returned with something that can never be taken away: an experience. This trip is so symbolic, and certain to be fraught with emotion . . . traveling to get a baby; I am sure there will be much to write about, and bought an extra-large notebook so I will be sure to have enough pages.

I like to look at the picture of the baby. Last night, when I showed it to my husband, he said, "She's the cutest thing I've ever seen! Why don't you bring one back for us, too?" He was obviously joking, but for some reason, I got angry.

"You can't just *do* that," I said. "You can't just bring back a baby." I wonder now if my anger was a telltale sign of a desire to do just that. I wonder if seeing these orphaned babies will make me want to have one too. Just yesterday, when I was having breakfast with a friend, we were talking about the trip and I said, "I'm really glad it's not me bringing home a baby!" And I am glad, for now, that it is not me.

I am still waiting for a burning desire for a child to come upon me, to feel that almost nonnegotiable need to have a baby that so many women experience. The longing for a child, to give birth, has never manifested for me in any significant way. In my early twenties I married a divorced man with three young children, and the role of stepparent has been difficult for me. And now, for the first time in fourteen years, my husband and I are poised at the beginning of something new: a life and marriage not dominated by children.

And though I have not arrived at any conclusions about having children of my own, I was excited for Alex when she first told me of her intention to adopt. She called me last summer, and after chatting about our lives for a few minutes, she paused and then said she had something to tell me. Her voice was serious, like she had bad news to impart, but instead, she said, "We've decided to adopt. We've already gone through the home study and are completing the paperwork. We'll probably have a child in a year or so, from China."

I was surprised, and told her so; she had never mentioned that she was thinking about adopting. "I've been thinking about it for a long time, and I decided if I don't do it soon, we'll be too old. We're already too old to adopt from South Korea, which was my first choice because they bring the babies to the U.S. and you don't have to travel to a foreign country."

She told me she had then selected China, because there were mostly girl babies available, and they were healthy. "I don't know why, but I keep seeing a little girl at the dinner table with us," she said. "A little girl . . . it has to be a girl."

"It's wonderful," I said then, and I am still happy for her, even though right now she doesn't seem very happy herself.

The day before we left, she called and told me that she had "freaked out" the night before. She had been preparing the nursery and suddenly was overcome with the need to run from the room, from the house, from her life.

"I've never felt that way before," she said. "Never felt that desperate."

"What do you think that was about?" I asked her, concerned. She told me it had taken several hours to calm herself down, and that she was sure it was just exhaustion, concern over the details of the trip and the adoption, and last-minute jitters. She hadn't been sleeping well, she said, and had a lot on her mind. "I'll be okay," she said. "I just need to get this trip behind me."

But the effects seem to be lingering. She is definitely not herself. Several times I have tried to engage her in conversation, to no avail. I brought a book for her called *Baby Signs*; a colleague of mine at the mental health agency where I used to work as a psychologist gave it to me, enthusiastic about the implications for parent-child interaction. I explained to Alex that experts now believe that babies can be taught to communicate fully using hand signals. The idea is that even infants have a sophisticated understanding of the world, that all that is lacking is the means to communicate.

"This might be good for you and your new baby because she won't understand English at first," I said. "It could help you to bond." She took the book and said, "Yes, that's interesting," and then tucked it away in a bag under her seat, not interested at all.

For a year and a half, Alex and her husband have been going through the arduous process of international adoption—a marathon of paperwork, red tape, and delays. She had not spoken much about the adoption since she first told me about it, and when she called six months ago to ask if I would go with her to China, I was more than a little surprised.

"Would you consider going to China with me, to pick up the baby?" she asked. She was not yet matched with a child, she went on before I could answer, but she and her husband were making decisions about the trip and she needed a companion. They had decided that he would stay home to care for their eight-year-old son.

"We don't want to take him out of school for ten days; plus, it's too long of a trip for him," she said.

When she asked again, would I come with her to China, I heard myself saying yes before even thinking. It would be an exciting adventure, another country to add to my list of places in the world that I had seen with my own eyes, and a chance to see how this business of international adoption actually works.

Alex and I have known each other for years, and yet, I would not consider us close. We met as neighbors, and ours was a social friendship; we saw each other a few times a year, at dinner with our husbands or in groups with other friends. We bonded initially because of shared circumstances: when we met, we had both recently become stepparents, and we talked often about the difficulties inherent in that role. Neither one of us had other friends who were stepparents at the time, and we became a sort of touchstone for each other when either of us needed to discuss some aspect of family life. Our families celebrated birthdays and holidays together on occasion; but there is something about Alex, a reserve or detachment, that I have never felt I could breach. In some sense she has remained aloof and un-knowable, an enigma, a mystery.

And then to ask me this, to go to China . . . After my initial positive reaction, I began to have reservations. This trip is so important; I asked Alex if there was a family member or a very close friend who could provide the kind of support necessary. What I meant, but didn't say, was "Why me?" Would our friendship withstand the intimacies of travel, not to mention an adoption? In some ways, I could rationalize this as a continua-tion of our support of each other around the issues of stepchil-dren, children, and family life. But in a deeper sense, I felt that this request pushed outside the bounds set for the relationship.

Alex explained that she had asked me to come because she needed an experienced traveler to go with her, someone who would not easily be thrown off stride. She had heard tales of my travels over the years, the places I had visited sometimes on a whim—the long trips by myself to Europe and South America. This is what she explained, but I had the sense that, deep down, even she did not know why she had chosen me.

She had settled on my travel history as her reason, but what she did not know was that my trips were not travel for the sake of travel alone, but always a looking, a searching for something, some piece of myself. My life had been made up of attempts to bury an old self, a person who no longer existed, a person who perhaps never existed, a self patched together from borrowed ideas. My trips were a way to tunnel into the dark country in-side myself, a place I could visit only when I was outside the ge-ographic bounds of my day-to-day existence.

It dawned on me the day Alex called, a day after I returned from a trip that had exhausted me and left me depressed, that perhaps looking for a piece of myself in some far-off location might not make much sense. Was travel just an escape, a way of fooling myself into believing that my life was moving forward when in fact it was standing still?

A vague sense of emptiness, of something missing, of not being where I should be, had haunted me for a lifetime. I was ready to admit that travel had not cured me, that nothing had cured me. The day before Alex called, I had decided to stay put for a while, to try living inside the life I had created in my suburban house, with my husband, my dogs—and my chronic discontent, the source of which I had yet to identify.

"It" eluded me, the "it" that would pull the world together and show that the world made eminent sense. I was looking for an answer, searching for a system, grasping at this and experimenting with that, but nothing coalesced, nothing calmed my spirit for long. As my discontent became more entrenched, as it became like a sort of grief, I began to panic . . . what was it, what was it, what was it? I did not know, and I began to think there might not be an answer, that maybe there were no answers at all. I had a growing sense that life was moving on and my dreams were dying. My life stretched out before me, a wasteland of time.

_∽_

After landing in Tokyo, we exit the plane silently and move into the terminal. Almost at once I am hit with a strong wave of nausea; I feel as if I'm going to pass out. Somehow I make it through the corridor to our gate, and then I have to sit down against a pillar and put my head between my legs. My mouth is watering profusely; I know if I move I will vomit.

This happens as soon as we enter the terminal and are met with a sea of Asian faces. Unfamiliar writing in Japanese characters on the signs above our heads, the singsong jumble of Asian languages filling the air around us; I become acutely aware of a feeling of being cut off from the world as I know it.

A virtual wave of humanity moves toward us in the corridor, and for some reason, this is a shock to my system. I feel a surge of energy hit me in the gut, and I become disoriented and weak. I am feeling this strange sense of fear, not just discomfort but anxiety, an anxiousness; it's as if I were in danger. It is irrational, and I don't mention it to Alex. She has enough on her mind right now so I suffer in silence.

The dream I had on the plane . . . the Asian faces surging down the corridor toward me. They swirl together and I can feel the earth spinning wildly beneath me, and for all I know it is wobbling off its axis. I hold my knees tightly and keep my eyes closed, praying for this to pass. The images unfold, and suddenly, I am back there in the dream:

I reached the gate that led to the garden of Black Dragon Pool, a secluded place where no one came, where no one ever came to witness the great beauty in which it lay. Beyond the gate something of priceless value awaited, and I had to reach that spot where I might be saved. Heaving open the heavy black lacquered gate, I fell inside and lay for a moment, spent with exhaustion. The wind moved gently through the trees, it sang to me of peace. I felt my breathing slow and my heart become calm as the wind caressed my skin and tickled the grass on which I lay. I lifted my head slowly, the reflecting pool was just ahead, not far away, I had to go there, I had to find an answer in its depths.

I have no memory of walking toward the water, but at once I was there, as if transported by my wish alone. On my knees at

its lip, I leaned over and parted the tall grass at its edge. I saw a
reflection rippling there, a face; but it was not mine! My mind
froze in confusion. I could not make sense of what I was seeing.
I looked hard and concentrated in order to bring the vision into
focus. A face . . . it was . . . it looked like . . . and then I realized
my prayers had been answered.

Later, when finally we left that place, hand in hand until
we reached the heavy black gate that led to the world, we peered
again into the depths of the reflecting pool. I noticed, floating in
its center, a lotus. It had not been there before, but now had
opened and spread its petals to the sun. A blessing, a pure white
reflection of the divine, it floated there serene and unassailable,
forever perfect.

I am in a dream, this is all a dream now and the way back home
is closed to me until I wake up. But into what reality will I
awake? In this moment nothing seems certain. I breathe, and
breathe; it is all I can do. For more than an hour I sit like this,
trying to hold it together, wondering if I'll be able to go on with
the trip.

Finally, our flight is called. Alex has to help me onto the
plane, which is packed with Japanese and Chinese businessmen. Except for the flight attendants, we are the only women
on this flight, and that makes me very uncomfortable. The men
don't acknowledge us at all; it is as if we were ghosts, we don't
exist. A distinctive smell emanates from these men; it has the
vague odor of hay that I remember from childhood visits to our
family farm. The smell makes me feel sick and I settle into my
seat and fall asleep right away, a deep, dense sleep, my mind
opaque, trying to escape. When I wake up we are landing in
Beijing, and my first thought is, What have I done?

It is dark when we land in Beijing, and flurries of snow swirl outside the window and across the tarmac. A set of stairs is wheeled up to the plane, and standing just outside the doorway as I am about to descend, I experience a wave of déjà vu. This scene looks so familiar, and it takes a moment to realize that I am remembering something I saw long ago. It is the image in my mind of former President Richard Nixon's visit to China, his arrival, nearly thirty years before. I saw it on television and in news photos, the fat flurries of snow, men in drab green military uniforms scurrying about with dour expressions on their faces, hurrying to accomplish some unknown, probably sinister purpose. Where have these memories been stored for all this time? In some dusty drawer of my mind, which has been waiting for just the right moment to spring open and display its contents.

Perhaps if that visit had never occurred, I would not be arriving in Beijing today, and somehow my subconscious mind has tied the two events together. I muse on the fact that every seemingly isolated event has repercussions through time. President Nixon's choices, decisions, and policies are affecting me some thirty years later, in a way he could never have conceived of at the time.

The terminal inside is nearly empty, yawning and eerily vacant. Though modern, clean, and brightly lit, it has the feel of a mausoleum. I have the feeling we are being watched. Going through customs and having my passport scrutinized by someone holding a gun unnerves me. I watch a skinny old man as he moves a dirty mop in slow circles around the floor. At eight o'clock on a Friday night, the airport of our nation's capital would be chaotic with travelers, but there is hardly anyone here.

Alex and I stand alone as the empty baggage terminal goes around and around. When we finally see our bags, it is a relief and we tug them off the belt and move uncertainly toward the exit. Now what? We scan the crowd, looking for the representative of the Chinese adoption service that works in tandem with the adoption agency back home. We spot a young woman holding a sign with Alex's name on it. She is from the China Women's Travel Service and will be our guide for this trip. She wears round glasses and has a shy demeanor; her hair is cut in a choppy chin-length shag. She tells us to call her "Anna," though that is obviously not her real name. She speaks excellent English. She helps us load our bags into a small white van parked at the curb; we drive off into the night, into a huge and strangely quiet city.

During the drive, Anna tells us that the two other couples in our group, who are also adopting, have already arrived at the hotel. Tomorrow we will visit the Great Wall, she informs us, and the next day, the Forbidden City. After that, we fly on to Nanchang, where we will meet the babies. A giddy excitement starts to return; this will be a grand adventure. I'm feeling much better now, since I slept on the flight from Tokyo. I stare out the window at the dark streets, looking for any type of life, and though I see none, I know it exists. Right now China is hiding, and tomorrow I will begin to find her.

⟊

I was to be a virgin bride for the Emperor, a bride he chose for himself while riding through the fields that surround my village on the way to a military engagement. He came upon me there, spoke to me from the back of his giant black steed. I said not a word; I was too shy to respond to his queries. He asked my age and my father's name, to which I re-

sponded with silence. But my eyes must have flashed, for he looked into them for a long moment before he rode off across the countryside with his guards and soldiers trailing behind. I ran home, breathless, to my father, legs bare since I had tied the hem of my garment into a knot at my hip. I had been flying my kite, hair loose and free; I knew I had to run with the wind, though the village women shook their heads and clucked their tongues at my behavior.

My beloved friend Chen had been with me in the fields, and now he followed behind, lurking outside my father's door as I recounted the story of my meeting with the Emperor. Father looked at me for a long while with a sad expression, and then said, "Run along now and start our dinner; it will soon be the end of the day." And he walked past me out of the house without looking at Chen standing just outside the doorway.

I told Chen to go too, as I had work to do. Chen had a sad expression just like my father's, and I did not want to see it anymore. "We'll meet tomorrow as usual," I told him, and gave him a smile and a pat on the cheek. We will be together always, I thought, in this little village. It made me happy to think of life in that way.

~

Waking to the sounds of voices in the hallway, something I cannot understand. "We will be together always." Is it possible I heard those words? The voices have a singsong quality, they rise and fall, getting louder as they approach, and then fading away until all I can hear is the sound of breathing coming from somewhere close by. Looking to the source of the sound, I see Alex in the next bed, still sound asleep. It seems like only minutes ago that I lay down on the hard twin bed in this room, last night around midnight, but I look at the clock and it is six o'clock in the morning.

I lie in the silence and think of the dream I was having just before I awoke, just before I heard the voices. A young Chinese girl, in a village . . . her father; she was upset, she was being sent away from him, to be a concubine, and she was desperate not to go. But it was me. . . . Was it me? Or someone else? It seems I was seeing the dream from behind her eyes. I shiver a little as I get out of bed and go to the window; I pull the nubby curtains open enough to see a slice of dull orange-gray sky, the sky of dawn in Beijing.

∽

It is early morning and we are driving to the Badaling section of the Great Wall, through the traffic-choked streets of Beijing. The van inches through the clogged intersections, trying to break clear to the outskirts of town to the tourist point two hours beyond. There are cars and trucks lined up bumper to bumper in each direction and on every road; it doesn't seem possible for anything to move. The smell of exhaust and gasoline is thick and strong, making me feel nauseous, irritating the lining of my nose and mouth. I wonder how the pedestrians and bicyclists can stand breathing all these fumes. There are thousands of bicycles zooming in and out of the traffic, darting between lanes, jumping up over curbs, and most are laden with some sort of cargo: a piece of furniture, live animals, lumpy bags that hold God knows what. I wonder what will happen with the already unmanageable pollution and traffic when all these people can afford cars.

Anna is singing. It is a song about a Chinese girl who lost her beloved, a man who dies while being forced to help in the building of the Great Wall. Anna explains that the girl, distraught, travels across the countryside, looking for her love, whom she never finds. She ends up dying at the Wall herself, and is buried inside. Anna tells us that the Wall was built to keep out invading armies. It never did. Instead, it served as an invitation to invasion, rather than a deterrent, because building a wall indicates weakness, a perceived vulnerability to attack. And once built, the separation and isolation that the wall enforces weakens the society further. To an enemy, the Wall was like blood in water to a shark, it whetted the appetite.

We gathered with the travel group in the lobby first thing this morning, and reintroduced ourselves. We had met the two other couples only once before, at the travel meeting at the adoption agency six weeks ago. Jimmy and Louise's daughter, Maggie, was with them this morning, returning to China for the first time since she'd been adopted five years before. Six years old and in high spirits, she ran up to us as if she had known us all her life, breathlessly reporting through her missing front teeth that we were all going "thight-theeing."

The other couples have been in China for several days, touring various sights and getting a feel for the country, and they are gushing about their tour of the Summer Palace. I listen with avid attention; I regret that there is so much I will not see and experience on this trip. "I'm not spending one extra day there," Alex had said when the subject of extending the itinerary came up at the travel meeting. "I just want to go, get the baby, and get out." Judy and Curtis are sitting in the seat behind me, and they begin describing their tour.

"It was a long climb," says Judy, "but then the view was of the entire Forbidden City. It was spectacular; it gave me chills!"

"I got it all on tape!" adds Curtis, swinging the camcorder he grips in his palm. Maggie runs to him and sticks her tongue out, and he immediately raises the camcorder and turns it on, recording the scene. Alex watches her from her seat across the aisle from me. She leans forward, toward me.

"Isn't she adorable?" she says in a semi-whisper.

"Perfect," I reply, nodding. "She would make anyone lose their doubts about adopting, if they had any."

Alex nods, mouths "Absolutely" as Anna starts singing another song.

"This song, about beautiful butterfly!" she says with a pleased smile, sure she is offering us something of great value. The way that she so unselfconsciously sings to us is endearing. It is something that a little girl would do. It indicates a naïveté, innocence, and lack of cynicism that is refreshing. An American, of the great entertainment society, might do this in a similar situation, but it would be a jokey thing, staged and false. Anna is offering herself; she is wide open, unprotected. Perhaps we are witnessing just that part of the Chinese character that so needed a wall.

Anna's singing turns an ordinary drive into a festive occasion. We are a little family, riding in a nondescript minivan, though we don't really know each other. Anna; Alex and I; Judy and Curtis; Louise, Jimmy, and Maggie; plus the driver . . . we have been brought together under unusual circumstances. A most intimate act, the adoption of a child—the creation of new families—being carried out among virtual strangers. And these adopting parents all seem so different from one another: Jimmy and Louise, working-class people from West Virginia; Judy and Curtis, government employees who live in D.C.; and Alex, a registered nurse, who didn't bring her husband at all.

What are they all doing here, I wonder. What forces have brought them to this place? Though on the surface they all share a desire to adopt a child, what underlying reasons have guided them here, to China, rather than to one of the numerous other countries where they might do the same? The process of adopting internationally is so lengthy, expensive, and intense, that to be finally here, thousands of miles from home, in a very foreign and until very recently closed society, speaks to the motivation needed for their quest. These are the most committed of prospective parents; perhaps they are not fully aware of what has driven them, or what lies ahead. But they are here, and in a sense, to me, this gives their lives a mythic dimension. No longer Curtis and Judy, the government employees, or Louise and Jimmy, housewife and contractor from West Virginia; but now, they are rescuers, redeemers, heroic and generous spirits, who have braved untold difficulties to recover the golden child. And yet, I don't sense that they see themselves in this way at all. It is fascinating to me, and I hope to have a chance to delve into these questions, to speak to these people about their lives and this decision before this trip is over.

Louise and Jimmy sit on the long bench across the rear of the van, and try to contain Maggie, who flits from person to person, sprinkling her charm among us all. This makes her parents uncomfortable, and every few minutes, one of them feels compelled to say, "Maggie! Come back here!" Or "Maggie, sit down, you're bothering people," even though she clearly is not. Having Maggie here to interact with is reassuring for these parents, like a fast-forward into the future, a preview of what their own child might be like. She reminds everyone why we are here.

Maggie comes to the front of the bus and wants to sing into the microphone. She is gorgeous, funny, and smart, a poster child for Chinese adoptions. She has been teasing Curtis throughout the trip and she has enraptured him with her natural charm. He keeps filming her with his camcorder, and though she is Chinese by blood, her actions are completely American. She is a performer, and wants us all to respond with approval, with praise.

Anna and Maggie alternate their musical offerings, and the contrast could not be more stark. Anna with her songs of lost loves and ancient China, sung in her high clear voice; Maggie with her selections of tunes from Sunday school and TV, belted out with gusto in a husky alto. I almost regret it when we finally reach the entrance to the Great Wall tourist point, so entertaining is the show.

We pile out of the van and it is so cold, the wind whips our faces. I pull my hat down over my ears, and suddenly I am alone in my own silent world. Small trinket shops line the walkway—you can buy T-shirts and stuffed pandas, jade and chopsticks, any kind of thing that will collect dust once you get it home but that seems like a good idea at the time. Red flags fly from a high archway over the road, their frantic flapping not festive but alarming. They make me think of danger; they are red daggers in the cold. We move quickly, but separately, like deep-sea divers who can see each other but cannot communicate except with hand signals. The cold takes our breath away and drives between us, but we regroup at the entrance and Anna shouts over the wind that we should meet back at this spot in one hour, pointing with exaggerated gestures at her wristwatch.

Alex and I climb the stairs leading to the Wall, together, silent. The stairs are steep and when we reach the top of the first section, a vast barren landscape spreads out before us, and in all directions, rolling brown hills and leafless trees. The bright sunshine has no warmth, but infuses everything with a brittle sharp luminescence, throwing harsh shadows in its path. We continue along the Wall, and it is surprising how steep it is;

you don't so much walk the Wall as climb it, like a mountain. At intervals there are stone staircases crowned by parapets where you can stop and take in the view, which is stunning at every point. To see a structure of this length and height snaking along the spine of this stark countryside, rising impossibly from out of nowhere, leaves me speechless. The sheer manpower needed to construct it is incalculable, and then to think that all that effort was futile in its purpose. The Wall reminds me of a grand loneliness and painful separation, a cleaving of the land and a cleaving of China from the world.

A sadness that I can't explain rises up in me with each step. Perhaps it has to do with the dream of last night, a strange dream in which something terrible happened that I was powerless to stop. In it I was a young girl, being taken from the only home I had ever known, a small village in a rural area. There was the sensation that I was riding for a long while in a carriage, and the countryside through which I passed looked a lot like the landscape that surrounds the Wall: empty, monochromatic, unwelcoming. There was someone else in the carriage with me on the journey, a young man; perhaps my brother or a friend? His face comes before my mind's eye, a smiling Chinese face. He was trying to comfort me . . . and then the memory of what happened at the end of our dream journey emerges:

Passing through the gates of the Imperial Palace was like entering another world. The immense wooden gates, painted blood red, the color of luck, the color of the empire, opened to allow our carriage to pass into the cloistered interior, and when they closed behind us with a thud that resonated throughout the courtyard, I felt a sudden wave of panic, of claustrophobic fear, which overwhelmed me and caused me to claw my nails into the palm of Chen's hand. His own hand returned the pressure, and I turned to look into my friend's eyes. We did not speak, for the air was filled with a noisy clamor, the bustle of court life, which was indifferent to our arrival.

In time the carriage came to a stop. The guard put his head in through the carriage door. He said, "Come out!" and I moved to rise from the bench, but my legs, so long immobile and shaking from fear, gave way beneath me. Chen turned and caught my arm to steady me, and our eyes met, uncertain and questioning. "It will be all right!" I said, to myself, to Chen. And yet a dread had begun forming, a knot of amorphous fear, the source of which I could not name. The excitement of new adventures and dreams of a new life seemed far away, as far as my father's house in the village, as untouchable as dream mountains shrouded in mist. I stepped forward toward the lip of the carriage, took the hand the guard offered, and descended to the dusty cobblestones in my poor cloth shoes that had been made for me in the village.

The poor cloth shoes . . . I can see them looming up before me as dream symbols sometimes do, their outline becoming sharper and more distinct, giving the impression that their significance transcends the dream narrative somehow, that if I could understand the message of this one object, the entire meaning of the dream would become crystal clear.

"Hey, let me take your picture!" suggests Alex, and I turn to give her my camera as the dream images slip away. I stand and pose, one hand on the ancient stones of the wall, stones that some unknown Chinese hand once placed here with great care. The past is tangible, and as close as my fingertips, yet impossible to grasp.

We continue on and I take photographs, knowing they will never capture the essence of this place. Alex and I walk the Wall for that hour, not speaking much, underdressed for the cold, and yet when we reach the steps to the plaza where we are to meet the others, I tell Alex to go on without me. I want to linger a moment, take some final shots with my camera, and try to discover what exactly it is that I am feeling. Alex moves on to the trinket shops, and I turn and place my hands upon the stone and look out over the rolling countryside. I close my eyes, breathe in the cold air, and focus on that breathing until my mind is as clear as the crystalline sky. There is a question inside me that will not quite form into words, and so I wait, willing to allow it to remain, for now, unasked.

ᦇ

The van crawls through the evening rush hour of Beijing. I have been lost in my thoughts the entire drive back, exhausted from the hike and trying to absorb the experience. I watch people outside the window, people on bicycles, people walking with huge bundles lashed to their backs, and people pushing carts laden with jumbles of cargo. Not one Caucasian face do I see, no blond hair, no blue eyes. I think of other foreign capital cities where I have seen a raucous mix of ethnicity, but not here.

There are modern buildings alongside dilapidated shacks. I see a man selling something from a steaming pot in front of a Western-style bank. I catch a glimpse of a woman inside a brightly lit storefront; it seems to be a beauty shop. The woman is young, dressed in sophisticated black, her hair beautifully coiffed. She is stunning; her face arrests my attention as we roll slowly past. She would not look out of place in Paris, or New

York, especially with the bored and jaded expression she expertly wears. Just past this shop, I see a woman walking in her drab gray Mao jacket and dusty shoes; she smiles and she has no teeth. Then and now, sharing the same sidewalk.

I am so tired, hungry, and cold. Jet lag has begun to take its toll. When we reach the hotel, I go straight to my room and to bed, and once I lie down, I cannot move. It is as if something has pinned me there. I drift in and out of sleep, beyond exhaustion, yet overstimulated. The Wall . . . fragments of Chinese songs . . . people's faces that I saw from my window . . . all move through my mind, a whirling ballet of images. At some point I hear Alex moving around the room, and I hear her say it's time to leave. We are scheduled to attend a Chinese opera performance. I hear her but am so tired I can't respond, and after she goes, I fall into a deep cavernous sleep, into a land of palaces and pagodas, dreaming of some time in China's past that seems like my own.

⁓

As the chanting gained in intensity, I felt a strong pull, as if I were being sucked into a tunnel, a tunnel of light. I could not resist but I was not afraid. Everything around me swirled and churned for what seemed like eternity. Suddenly I saw before me a face, a smiling face, and the swirling stopped. It was a face I had seen before, one of the monks who chanted in the courtyard each morning. I could still hear the chanting, as if in the distance, but I was so focused upon this face hovering before me that all else disappeared. The monk looked into my eyes with an expression of profound kindness. When he spoke it was as if the voice were disembodied: the lips did not move, the expression did not change. And yet I heard clearly the kind monk speaking to me. He said, "And so, you are ready?" Without my thinking of it, my answer rose up, "Yes, I am ready, Master," but I did not know how or why I spoke thus. This seemed to please him, for he smiled broadly and said, "I will help you." And the vision evaporated before me. I stood at my doorway for some time after the monks filed back to their chambers. I could not make sense of what had just occurred. Was I imagining things? Or dreaming? Had I fallen asleep during the chanting? The vision was so real, I felt I could reach out and touch it. As the vision faded, I felt weak and depleted. I wanted it back. I wanted to see the kindly face again. But no matter how hard I tried, I could not produce the image again in my mind. It had vanished like the smoke from the incense, leaving only a question. What had just happened to me, what did it mean?

It was then that my musings were interrupted by a commotion in the courtyard. I looked up to see a group of the Emperor's men in the distance, moving toward me. The men were dressed in the elaborate uniforms of the court, with long brocade robes and towering head-dresses that from a distance gave the men the illusion of being very tall. As they approached, I could see that the men were dragging someone, someone who appeared to be struggling mightily to escape from their clutches. Soon they were directly in front of my chamber doorway and they stopped for a moment as the struggle from the captive became fiercer and fiercer. Several of the men had sticks and were bringing them down harshly upon the back, legs, and torso of the person being dragged, but this seemed to do little to subdue his struggle. Then suddenly, the knot of men opened for a brief moment in the confusion and gave me a clear and unobstructed view, and I could see that it was Chen. It was Chen, my beloved friend, being dragged, being struck, being taken somewhere against his will.

I stifled a scream along with the words that rose into my throat, "No! What are you doing? Leave him be, leave him be!"

I wake with the sensation that I have just been falling. What time is it, isn't there something I should be doing, or should have done? The clock says eight a.m.; I have been asleep for fifteen hours. I sit up, look over, and see that Alex has rolled over, with her back to me, on her bed, still asleep. The last thing I remember is that she was getting ready to go out with the group, to the opera performance.

I get out of bed and move to the window, pull back the dingy curtain, and sit on the cold metal ledge with my notebook and pen. There was a dream last night, and for the time being I can remember it from beginning to end. Another dream about China . . . I need to scribble it down before it fades away, like the morning mist above the rooftops of Beijing.

The sun is trying to find a reason to shine today, through the gloom of pollution haze. A sea of continuous rooftops spreads out before me, punctuated here and there by an interior courtyard, where I can glimpse the mundane activities of daily life. A man is walking, holding a cage, inside is a live chicken. I watch as he turns in to one of the narrow alleys, and then a few moments later he emerges into the courtyard of a house and sets the cage down, and then disappears. Dinner for this evening, still alive this morning, but certainly not for long.

This is not a beautiful city. Even in the pristine stillness of dawn it seems dirty and sad. I notice five birds circling in the air above the rooftops. They circle the same patch of air, moving higher and higher in a slow, elegant maneuver. Up in a spiral, and then lazily down again to alight on one particular rooftop, all in a row. Moments pass, and the cycle repeats, the birds taking off into flight, performing this silent air ballet. Someone has trained them, has spent many hours shaping their natural grace into something of even greater beauty, and I find comfort in this. At least one patch of this chaotic cityscape was made beautiful by the hand of man, by intention.

The strange night of dreams has left me disoriented. Catching hold of fragments here and there . . . a courtyard, a group of monks . . . what was it? I was in a place I did not recognize, from another time, ancient Imperial China. I write:

> *I am watching as a group of monks is praying in a courtyard. They are chanting in a language I do not understand. One of the monks appears before me and speaks; he is going to teach me, and asks if I am ready. I tell him that I am, and call him "Master." Just then I see a group of soldiers carrying another man toward a doorway and I know it is either my friend or my brother and they are going to do something terrible to him. They carry him by the arms and legs, and hit him brutally as he struggles to get free. In the dream, I know that they are taking him away to castrate him so he can become a eunuch. I scream but it is no use. I fall to the ground in despair and lie on the cold ground for what seems like an eternity. Then I hear the monk, the one I called "Master," say, "Come to me."*

"Come to me." What could that mean? This dream seems beyond any type of Freudian analysis, a favorite pastime of mine. It is a story, like watching a movie, but the feelings are so real that it's as if I actually lived it.

My dreams are becoming more and more like this; they are whole and resist reduction. All my life I have been a prolific dreamer, but in the last few years, many of my dreams have been continuations of dreams I had in the past. I am living another lifetime in the night. Sometimes it takes the entire next day to recover my bearings, and the "real" world of my daily life often pales in comparison to my dream experiences.

I close my notebook and start to dress, looking for my running shoes amidst the clutter of our suitcases. There is a gym downstairs in the hotel, and I run for three miles on the treadmill, listening to Chinese rock music blaring over the stereo, staring at a blank wall and trying to figure out what the lyrics might mean. A young male attendant stares at me the entire time with a blank expression, which at first makes me uncomfortable and self-conscious; after a while, I don't even notice.

An hour later we meet the others in the lobby and begin loading the bags into the van before climbing in ourselves. Today we are visiting Tiananmen Square and the Forbidden City, which is one of the main reasons I wanted to come on this trip. These icons of a foreign culture loom large in my imagination, like the Eiffel Tower or the Coliseum, like Buckingham Palace or the Kremlin. Pictures never do these things justice, one can never know what a landmark truly represents until one stands before it, until it is seen in the context of its surroundings.

When I caught my first glimpse of the Eiffel Tower, I cried, and not because the beauty of it overwhelmed me. I cried because I was seeing it from afar, above the rooftops of an industrial slum outside Paris, from the window of a bus I was riding from Charles de Gaulle airport into town. From that perspective it looked ugly and pointless, so incongruous against the backdrop of run-down apartment buildings and factories belching smoke. This is the celebrated symbol of Paris, I thought, steel scaffolding serving no purpose? The actual sight of it punched a hole in the fantasy bubble I had created, and from then on, I looked at pictures of all such icons with skepticism, withholding judgment until I could see them for myself.

During the ride to the center of town, I am again amazed by the people coming and going, on bicycles piled with pots and pans, crates, chickens, children, or whatever needs transporting. The riders weave in and out of the vehicular traffic with the boldness of experienced daredevils. Riding to work or the market, purposeful and without a moment to waste, oblivious to the danger or accepting it as part of the price of daily life. These people appear to meet the mundane challenges of daily living with flair.

The van stops along a busy thoroughfare, and we pile out and assemble on the sidewalk directly across from a huge two-story McDonald's restaurant on the edge of Tiananmen Square. The golden arches bracket one side of the square, while a huge portrait of Chairman Mao smiles from the other. East and West, each holding its ground while keeping a sharp eye on the other, staring each other down.

As we walk closer to the square, my excitement builds as it starts to sink in where we are, this historic place. I keep saying to anyone who will listen, "Do you believe we're here? Do you believe we're here?" because I can't, it is surreal. I think of the tanks rolling through this square, mowing down the students who had staged a protest calling for democracy. I think of the staged military parades and the Communist leaders waving to the rows and rows of soldiers from their viewing stand, high above the fray.

Tiananmen Square is the symbol of modern China, as the Forbidden City is the symbol of ancient China, and it is a surprise to me how they nestle up against each other. Somehow, I had not imagined they would be so close in proximity. Tiananmen is a vast space, much larger than I expected, and though the expanse is so large and open, there is an unmistakable feeling of entrapment. Once again I have the feeling we are being watched.

Every soldier in the square, and there are many, carries a large gun over his shoulder or strapped to his waist, a reminder that we are really just fish in a barrel, easy targets.

We walk through the square, taking pictures here and there. I snap one of Alex as she stands smiling in front of the tall obelisk that is a monument to "the people."

"Should I take one of you with your camera?" I offer.

"I didn't bring one," she replies sheepishly. Before I can say anything, she hastily justifies herself. "It was just one extra thing to carry."

"Didn't bring your camera!" I exclaim, truly surprised. Who would not bring a camera on a trip where they were adopting a child? I brought my camera, ten rolls of film, and a journal to record this momentous occasion; she brought nothing that might save the memories for later.

"Well, I knew you would bring one," she says. "I just thought I'd be too busy to take pictures."

She snaps one of me, with my camera, in front of the sign that keeps track of how many days to go until the territory of Macau returns to Chinese control. Everything in this square seems to be about reinforcing the idea that the Chinese government is in total control. There are no foreign tourists other than our group in the square this morning. There are also very few Chinese tourists, and the ones who are here are bundled up in large coats, hats, and scarves. No one speaks to us, as they had at the Wall yesterday. The most interesting people in the square are the soldiers, and I watch them, fascinated.

Judging by the hard expressions on their faces, wearing their drab green uniforms confers upon them a terrible burden. They attempt to hide this with arrogance as they patrol the square, pushing people around with their don't-mess-with-me attitudes. Most of the Chinese people here in the square ignore it, used to a lifetime of authoritarian rule. But for me, an American, it comes as a shock. It is an affront to my sensibilities; I feel a wave of disgust every time I look at one of their faces. Where in the United States would we see military personnel patrolling a public square like this, armed to the hilt? The disturbing aspect is that they are not here to protect the people; they are here to squelch any type of dissent aimed at the Communist party. There is no one to protect the people here, despite the monument erected in their honor. Their own government suspects them, spies on them, restrains them, and inhibits them, and they must toe the line. They must acquiesce because of the guns on the backs of their own young countrymen, who will do the bidding of the state against them. The soldiers' faces say they will, and I believe them.

Anna moves us along as we snap pictures in front of the giant smiling portrait of Chairman Mao that hangs above the entrance to the Forbidden City. I have read a bit about him, and his image gives me a feeling of unease. The cruelty he perpetrated, the repression of his people, is well known, and yet here he is, his influence still hanging over everything. He is fully present, the people yet unwilling to let him go. Mao Tse-tung, who controlled China for over twenty-five years, is still revered, despite having been responsible for the deaths of tens of millions of Chinese. And this is not ancient history: Mao ruled from 1949 until 1976, only yesterday in historical terms.

The past is so oppressive here in this ancient land, and perhaps the Cultural Revolution was an attempt to smash and destroy the burdens of time. But as is so often the case, one way of oppressing people is substituted for another, and the cycle continues, until oppression itself is seen as the real enemy, and all forms of it are rejected by a people. China's history, spanning thousands of years, is rich and varied; I often hear people speak of China reverentially, as being an "ancient culture" and thus worthy of awe or respect on that basis. But it is also true that as a thing ages, it can become decrepit, inflexible, and incapable of regenerating itself. Age or length of time in operation is no guarantee of wisdom or benevolence. Oftentimes, the older something is, the farther it is away from its ideal.

A throng waits at the entrance to the Forbidden City just underneath Mao's portrait, and we join the line of people waiting to get in. Suddenly, a commotion directly in front of us catches our attention. A group of people is sitting in a circle, holding hands, eyes closed in peaceful silence, surrounded by a crowd of onlookers. Sirens begin blaring in the distance, coming closer, the shrill sound piercing the air. The men in drab green finally have something to do, and they come rushing forward from all sides of the square, as if racing to put out a fire. They move in, violently parting the crowd, pushing aside anyone in their way— women, children, old people. They begin grabbing the arms of the meditators, screaming at them, ordering them to do something, to move, to obey. The circle of sitters does not move and the soldiers begin dragging them by whatever body part they can grab—hair, arms, legs; they are punching them and kicking them, though the meditators are not resisting. A police van comes screeching to a halt in front of the melee, and the soldiers start dragging, pushing, and stuffing the offending individuals into the van. One man shields his face from the blows of a nightstick, a woman holds her arm in pain as a soldier twists it behind her back. The crowd looking on makes no move of protest—the guns, after all . . . but I see no signs of revulsion or even surprise evident on their faces.

Anna hisses at us to keep moving, don't even look in that direction; and no matter what, do NOT take any pictures! We are shaken; we do as we are told. Our little group moves slowly past the scene, trying hard to stay together and not be separated in the crowd. Anna pulls us along, shepherding her flock to safety. We are all watching intently, cannot take our eyes off this scene. Jimmy holds Maggie in his arms, pushing her head down against his shoulder, protecting her from the sight of this violence. Judy looks ashen, and Curtis seems unsure of what to do, his camcorder useless, his arm limp at his side. None of us speaks. There is an almost embarrassed silence among us, like guests at a dinner party where the host has suddenly become belligerent to his wife.

Something is oddly out of balance here. I know now why these young men's faces are so hardened and immobile. If it were not so deadly serious, it would be almost comical, a farce. Skinny men barely out of their teens dressed in ugly uniforms, rushing around and hitting people on the head with nightsticks for sitting down and thinking. The insanity, the complete insanity of fear, is obvious here.

I look up at the smiling Mao. And you! You are dead now, but somewhere beyond, are you witnessing this? Are you proud of what you have wrought? I read somewhere that Mao was raised a Buddhist by a devoutly religious mother, whom he revered. He gave up religion in early adulthood, and when he came to power, he forced everyone else in China to give it up too. But things forbidden have a special lure, and it is clear by what we have just seen that religion has not been eradicated completely.

When we are at a safe distance and the shrill call of the sirens has died down, I turn to Anna. "What do you think of this? Does it bother you?" I ask. Her face goes slack, and she moves away a little, she doesn't want to talk. "Really, what do you think? Do you talk about this with friends, with family?" I press her, move toward her. The others are moving ahead, she is no longer at the head of her flock. Alex looks back and Anna gestures at her with her hand, move on. Anna looks around, side to side, and then steps closer to me, with a gesture of her hand that shows her practiced restraint.

"What can we do?" she says, and it is obvious to me that she feels she is taking a risk in answering me. "We just want to live our lives. If we protest, they'll arrest us, too; and we want to live!" she says, in a low, strained voice. I start to speak, I am set to argue, to say, "But then nothing will change!" The look on her face deflates my intention and I see, as she said, that it is no use. The Chinese have lived with this type of authoritarian system for thousands of years, both under the old empire and now under the Communists. For me, an American child of the sixties and seventies, this acceptance of powerlessness is unthinkable; and yet I see that here, perhaps acceptance is the intelligent thing, and protesting tantamount to suicide. It is the way things are. And in that moment, I see that even my questioning Anna along these lines is a dangerous thing. For her to have this kind of job, guiding Americans who are here to adopt babies, she must be in some way a trusted member of the establishment. Perhaps she had to profess loyalty to the Communist party many, many times in her life; and I am asking her to criticize it, and put herself and her job at risk. My first reaction upon seeing the arrests in the square was to assume that anyone would find the arrests and the state that sanctioned them abhorrent. But I had forgotten that it is possible that not everyone longs for free-dom. Some who have been imprisoned for long periods start to fear the outside world, preferring the comfort and security of the known.

My vehemence dies down and I think of the entire tableau that has just played out before me. Tiananmen Square . . . soldiers . . . Chairman Mao . . . people meditating . . . meditation? As a threat to the state? What exactly are they so afraid of, to unleash so much force for so little reason? The Chinese government seems to be acknowledging that meditation, which is a going within, a strengthening of the mind, is dangerous, and they are right. Mao himself would have known this, having been a Buddhist in his early years. True power for change starts within the individual, within the mind and heart. A free mind and heart is beyond the control of any government, and this freedom cannot be taken away, no matter what you do to the body. Throw it in jail, starve it, even kill it; it makes no difference. Meditation is a danger to any system that seeks to control others through fear, that seeks to maintain external power over others at any cost. And many minds, millions of minds, focused together on change, on freedom, on self-realization, would bring down this totalitarian government if the focus were sustained for any length of time.

These people, the ones just arrested, may be beyond being hooked by fear; but the ones watching, the ones who have not yet tasted the freedom that lies within, perhaps they can be frightened into believing that even beginning is dangerous or evil. I look at Anna's face and absorb her words, and it dawns on me that she knows this, she knows. I nod to her slightly and we move away from each other, and though we don't speak of it again for the rest of the trip, an invisible bond is now between us, a meeting of the minds.

Stepping through the doorway into the Forbidden City is like entering a place where time has stopped. After the melee of the arrest and the hubbub of Tiananmen Square, the empty silence of the imperial fortress is deathlike. Nothing lives here. I feel a chill as we begin walking across the first of the many open courtyards, and pull my thin coat more tightly around my body. The air is crisp and sharp, the cold is reaching into every part of me, covered and uncovered, until even my toes inside my heavy boots are numb.

We walk slowly through the courtyard, looking around, no one speaking, as if we have entered the hushed interior of a library. There is nothing to say, and I am having difficulty formulating complete thoughts. I think of a scene from the movie *The Last Emperor,* when the orange-robed monks fill the courtyard with chants as they bow before the new Emperor, only three years old. The little Emperor only wants to run through the ranks of the monks, to play hide-and-seek. That scene has stayed with me, though I saw the movie many years ago. It was the chanting of the monks that most affected me, and I can imagine the faint echoes of the tones as I stand here, in the now abandoned city.

Emperors lived here once, emperors and empresses. This is a vast, orderly, and spacious sanctuary that protected its occupants from the rest of the unruly city, and yet they must have been unhappy here, isolated as they were from the outside world. The buildings are beautiful, but I feel nothing. It is as if all traces of human energy have been somehow removed, and all that remains is a void.

The structures are grand in size and decoration. Intricate

carvings of animals and birds along the rooflines keep catching my attention, and I stop to photograph them, their sharp angles juxtaposed against clear blue sky. I move inside one of the pavilions—the rest of the group is standing just in front of a throne that has been roped off against tourist intrusion. I move up just as they start moving away; I feel forced to move on, though I would like to stay and absorb this place. The others seem distracted and uninterested in historical significance, and for good reason: tomorrow they will meet the babies, and it must be difficult to keep their minds on anything else.

"Dude had it made," declares Jimmy, gesturing at the throne, speaking of the Emperor. The others chuckle at this, but I say, "In the end he didn't!"

Anna turns to me and says, "What?"

"Never mind," I say, and she shakes her head as if to say, "I give up." Though her English is good, she doesn't understand slang, and oftentimes she is left wondering what someone in the group has said.

We move out of the pavilion, and from there we climb a set of stone steps onto a raised terrace, where we can look back to where we have just come from and see the vast rows of tiled rooftops that make up the buildings of the Forbidden City. It is here that I have the first sense that this is indeed a city of immense proportions. It is a wonder of design. I read in the visitors' center on the way in that the city is arranged along an axis, a spine, and the pavilions represent the seven energy chakra points of the body. As you move progressively from pavilion to pavilion, you move toward greater and greater power, until you reach the seventh, the crown chakra, the Emperor's throne. This is where he supposedly communed with the gods, but in the end, it did nothing to save him from "the people."

As the group moves through the site, I keep thinking of the people just arrested outside the Forbidden City. They were arrested for meditating. Actually, they were arrested for being members of a group deemed a "cult" by the Chinese government, as most religions have been. It is obvious that the cult that controls the guns has the power to designate which other cults are allowed to operate within the system. As Mao himself was quoted as saying, "Power comes from the barrel of a gun."

Just yesterday I meditated in the shadow of the Great Wall of China, and today I will do so within the walls of the Forbidden City. I will practice with a delicious sense of subversion, knowing that no one can stop me, and in a spirit of solidarity with those just arrested. I do not close my eyes as I usually do, to remain unobtrusive, and yet a young man in military uniform stops talking with his comrades and watches me as I stand away from the group, looking out over the courtyard. Something about me has alerted his attention, but as I am doing nothing that can be deemed inappropriate, he loses interest and begins talking again with his friends.

As my breath slows and my focus of attention shifts from the outer world to the inner world, I can still see everything that surrounds me, but also, at the same time, can see with my inner vision. Never before have I experienced this, to be fully aware of the external world and the internal world simultaneously, without effort. Perhaps it is this place, I think, this void, that produces a type of heightened perception:

There is an image, like a transparency that has been laid over my physical sight; I am seeing a woman lying on the ground. She does not move. She is dressed in an elaborate robe, which is arrayed around her body. I know she has been lying there for some time. No one comes to her, she is utterly alone. The woman is lying next to a garden wall, a very high stone wall. Suddenly I see something rising over the wall, something flutters and rises . . . it is a kite. It rises higher and higher. The woman on the ground stirs, she lifts her head and sees the kite high above her, and she jumps to her feet. She is sobbing as she runs to the garden wall. I can see her shoulders shaking and heaving. She reaches up—

A shout rips my attention from the inner scene and back to the courtyard below, and the scene fades entirely as I watch one of the men in military uniform throw something to the ground, a small package. His friends are laughing, their white teeth gleaming in the sunshine. The sound startles me back, and now I am fully present here, in the cold. I turn to look for the others, they have moved on toward the next pavilion, and I hurry to catch up to them.

I follow to the entrance of a walkway, next to which is a sign indicating that the area beyond is the place where the Emperor's concubines and wives were housed. A set of beautifully carved and painted doors sets the space apart, and as soon as I see them, an image from my dreams—perhaps it is from the night before last—comes to mind. The dream about the shoes . . . there was something about concubines in it as well; going to a place where they lived, and I was going to live there too? In the dream, as here, there was a set of elaborately carved doors that I had to enter, and as I pass through now, I look closely at the design of flowers, trees, and birds that covers the front panel of the doors.

Apparently the women were confined to this specified area and not allowed to roam freely in the Forbidden City, and only women and eunuchs were allowed to enter. Inside is a small courtyard surrounded on all sides by bedchambers and sitting rooms. In the center of the courtyard is a large, dark stone, encased in a glass box. A sign says that this stone symbolized the purity of the concubines. As I look at it through the glass, I wonder, did it absorb impurities from these women somehow? The stone has a presence, an energy still emanates from it, unlike anything else in this place. It must have been witness to centuries of intrigue, drama, heartbreak. . . . I feel a deep urge to touch the stone, to run my fingers over its variegated surface, but the glass prevents me, and I turn to wander around the courtyard, looking into the chambers, each one small, with a built-in bed covered in silk cushions—the focal point of the room, as it was the focal point of the inhabitants' lives.

They were called concubines, but they were slaves, imprisoned here to serve their master. The value of a woman was based solely on her ability to please one man; she was a commodity. How painful this must have been. I wonder how I would have adapted to such a system. Would I have gone along or tried to rebel somehow? It was a different time, a different society. . . . Would I have been conscious of the injustice, or is that mainly my modern-day sensibility layered over the past?

During my childhood, I had an innate and heightened awareness of unfairness and inequality, as many children do. But I especially chafed at the rules that applied only to girls and curtailed my natural desire for freedom. Boys were allowed to do things that I was not, even though I knew them to be no smarter than I, and no more courageous. I fought hard, competing with boys—in school, on the playground, and at home with my older brother. I resisted domination by anyone or anything, especially boys, and my mother always said that I'd had this type of fight in me from the moment of my birth. Where did that intensity come from, I always wondered, as it seemed out of proportion to the actual limitations imposed on me by my parents and society, as if I were driven by a reaction to an experience that predated my birth.

I wonder, if I had lived as a concubine in Imperial China, would I have suffered here, under this system, even if I had had no knowledge of modern ideas of gender and freedom? I listen hard as I hear the answer rise up from deep within: yes. Having no knowledge that freedom was possible would have made the suffering even worse, because there would have been no hope. Hope saves us from ourselves.

მ

Inside the gates of the Forbidden City, the Chinese tourists seem interested in us. There is an evident curiosity, and some even muster the courage to interact with us. They are especially interested in Maggie, a little Chinese girl accompanied by two tall blond, blue-eyed American parents. Several Chinese women ask to hear her speak; others bring their own Chinese babies and children to hug her and touch her hand, or have their pictures taken with her. It is as if Maggie were a lucky talisman, as if a child who touches her would receive some spark of her energy. It appears that this association with Americans or being an American is seen as desirable for most, although it is difficult to tell. At the Great Wall yesterday, when Alex and I were standing waiting for the others to appear, a group of high-spirited teenagers approached. One bold girl asked if she could stand next to us while her friend took our picture. Surprised, we agreed, and immediately two other girls jumped to either side of us before their young male friend snapped a picture. They were very excited about this, and chattered together, arms waving, laughing as they walked away from us.

"That was weird," Alex said, and it was. The incident made me uneasy and I had a feeling somehow that we had just been had, though I was not sure what it meant. I got the distinct feeling we were the butt of some joke they were pulling, but could not tell if the punch line was benign or malevolent.

We leave the Forbidden City and emerge once again to the sound of traffic and commotion in the heart of Beijing. It is a jolt, to be suddenly back in the modern world after spending hours in the relative silence and serenity inside ancient walls. A van is waiting just outside to take us directly to the airport for our flight to Nanchang. The sightseeing for the trip is over, and from now on everything on the schedule will revolve around the babies, starting tomorrow morning when they are to be delivered to their new parents at the hotel.

During the ride to the airport I watch the billboards and traffic outside my window, and think of how tonight I will write in my journal and try to make sense of the vivid dreams and meditation experiences of the last two days. A Burger King sign looms above the roadway where modern cars whiz past our van. This admixture of past and present, East and West, has me disoriented, and I suddenly feel so tired, tired to the bone. Alex and the others seem tired too; no one speaks during the ride, each person seemingly lost in his or her own thoughts. All I want to do is sleep, and two hours later, when I am settled into my seat aboard our flight, I do sleep, but I do not rest.

The monk leaned down and put his hand upon my head. A tingling feeling began from where he had placed his hand and spread down to my throat, to my chest, until my entire body felt alive and quivering. The fatigue disappeared, and I sat up, my mind clear as it had never been. Then I looked into his eyes. The dark eyes contained everything I needed, and I began speaking, telling the monk the story of my arrival here in the palace, of leaving my father's house in the countryside, of bringing Chen with me on this grand adventure, of my loneliness and fear. I told him too of my rising each morning to listen to the prayers of the monks, of that being my solace and peace in this strange, cold place. And finally, I told him of Chen, of the horror of what I feared had happened to my friend. And he listened as if he already knew.

"My child we have much work to do. All will become clear in time, and you will know the answers to your questions. But now, I want to tell you of something which will help you in your grief. Your friend has come to a crossroads, a place where his spirit must make a decision and a choice. Nothing is what it seems, my child, and everything that occurs can be used for growth if we so choose. All fear and pain are but illusions when you understand. And you can help your friend now only through the strength of your own spirit. What is it that you want? Go into the garden of your chambers and contemplate this question, go each day until the answer comes. When it comes, return to me, and we will begin."

And then I reluctantly left him. I would do as he said. I had nothing else, nothing else . . . and so for many days I went into the garden at sunrise and stayed until dusk, when the chill chased me to a fitful sleep on my small bed. Each day I asked the question of myself and each day I found no answer there. I kept thinking and wondering about Chen— Where was he? Had he lived or died? I knew that to become a eunuch a

*man had to undergo a painful butchery, and that many contracted
fevers or other illness or lost their spirit and became mere shadows. And
this when they had freely chosen this path. What of Chen, who was
forced into this drastic procedure? I knew him so well, knew he dreamed
of a family and children, knew of his pride and hopes. I was sick with
worry, so that each time I tried to contemplate the question posed to me
by the monk, my mind returned to grief, to Chen.*

*I had many dreams in the night—I saw the monk's face, I saw
Chen and spoke with him, I saw my father. And then one night I had a
dream that caused me to sit up with a gasp, so vivid and alive was the
experience. I saw Chen, beautiful Chen, and he was running in a field
of flowers. He was laughing and joyous, and behind him rose a mag-
nificent kite, a dragon, with a full tail of rainbow colors that whipped
mightily in the wind. Oh, and he was happy! My Chen, what I
wouldn't give to see you so again, and I sobbed and sobbed through
that night, not knowing how I could go on, not knowing if I wanted to.*

*That night was eternal, and in it, I began to pray. I prayed for re-
lease from this pain, for salvation, for something to make sense. My
pain was a wave so huge it could take me to heaven. I felt myself riding, spinning, falling, and all the time the question echoed, What do
you want, What do you want?*

*And when I fell into that sleep that is beyond sleep, the sleep of ex-
haustion of all hopes, I heard for the first time an answer, so small and
weak, and yet an answer nonetheless. What do you want, What do you
want? I want to live, was the answer; I want to live.*

∾

"What do you want?" I wake to see Anna, Alex, and the flight attendant who is standing in the aisle staring at me, waiting for a
reply. I think she has asked me if I want something to drink,
and I wave my hand no, I am fine, and they all look away from

me as I turn back to the window. I have just been dreaming again, and once more the setting was Imperial China, a palace there. It was something about a monk again, and making decisions that were of profound importance.

It must have been triggered by our visit to the Forbidden City, but it felt so real, what is going on with all these dreams? I check my watch. We have a little less than an hour before we land; I have time to write this down before I forget. I take out my notebook and begin writing in my journal, the journal that was meant to be a chronicle of my trip, but is now becoming a chronicle of a life being lived inside my dreams.

∽

An attractive young woman dressed in a Western-style business suit meets us outside the airport. She is competent and efficient, instructing porters where to take our bags, and guiding us to yet another van, which waits for us at the curb. She asks us to call her "Sheila," the Americanized name she has chosen to make it easier for us to address her. She never tells us her Chinese name, nor has Anna. They cannot be who they really are with us; they must alter their identities in an attempt to bridge the cultural gap for the time they are to spend as our guides. It must be a strain to do so, and several times I notice Sheila becoming impatient as she reads us the itinerary and tries to explain the schedule for our time in Nanchang.

At the front of the van, Sheila and Anna put their heads together and whisper, hands covering their mouths as they keep one eye on the parents in the back, conferring about details. They obviously know each other well, and Sheila wears a badge that says CHINA WOMEN'S TRAVEL SERVICE, the same organization for which Anna works.

We drive a long way through open fields on a highway that could have been in any modern country in the world. The land is flat and dull and dusty, uninteresting in every way, and I find it hard to stay awake as we drive, still half-caught in the world of my dreams. Someone with a kite . . . running in a field of flowers; the kite turned into a dragon . . . someone named Chen?

Sheila is passing out some papers for the adoptive parents to look at, and mentally I check out—it has nothing to do with me. Several moments and a few dusty miles later, I catch the tail end of a statement that startles me back to attention: did she just say the babies will be there at the hotel, today? All day long Anna has been telling us the babies will not be delivered to the hotel until tomorrow morning, and the parents set their minds to a relaxing evening with nothing on the schedule. Anxious as they all are to meet their new children, a nice meal and some sleep are what they were looking forward to for this evening. To suddenly think of dealing with babies in less than fifteen minutes, just off a plane, hungry, exhausted, and not prepared, is overwhelming for us all.

It is as if someone has thrown a switch inside the van, the air becomes electrified with anxiety. Jimmy stands up, and starts talking to Sheila in a loud voice, gesticulating with his hands and pointing to the papers she has given him. Louise puts her head next to Maggie's and says something to her; Maggie starts bouncing up and down in the seat, saying, "Yippee! Yippee!" and clapping her hands.

Judy looks as if she is hyperventilating. She puts her head down between her arms, which are resting on the seat back in front of her, while Curtis rubs her back helplessly. Alex, sitting next to me, looks green. Her hands flutter as she rifles through her briefcase full of papers, though there is no paperwork to be done.

"I can't believe this," she says. "I'm not ready! Oh my God."

"This is great!" I say, and she turns to me, a blank look on her face. Her eyes are glazed over, as though she's not really seeing me. Louise turns around, and I say, "What do you think?"

"We've been through this before," she answers, as if trying to reassure herself, not me. She turns back around, and tells the bouncing Maggie, "Settle down!"

Until this moment, the idea of the babies has been an abstraction for me, just part of this trip but not the entire reason I am here. Now that meeting them is imminent, an excitement surges through me, a sudden happiness that feels the way Christmas morning felt when I was a child, just before seeing what Santa brought. I cannot contain it, I start laughing, and clapping my hands like Maggie. Why, I ask myself, do I feel so excited, when I am not getting a baby? Probably, I reason, because the thought of being responsible for a baby for its lifetime is not intruding upon me as it certainly is for the parents. But still, the pure joy that wells in me is so unexpected—a vicarious happiness that feels entirely personal. In this moment I feel as if the babies are mine, too; and by the time we arrive in front of the Hotel Jin Feng, I can't wait to see them.

"Will they be in the lobby when we go in? Will we see them right away?" I ask Sheila as I step from the van.

"I don't know," she answers, distracted, not wanting to engage. The panicked reaction of the parents has thrown her off stride; she is trying to regain the authority she lost when the change of plans was announced, and is giving directions to each person as they emerge from the van.

Suddenly Maggie is beside me, and I reach down and grab her hand. She looks up with a beseeching smile, and I give her hand a squeeze as we walk inside through the big glass doors.

The new parents are all hanging back, and I want to run in, to look for babies, for people holding babies. There is something in this, the idea that human babies are being brought here to be "given" to these people, who have come from so far away. In my mind somehow, in my imagination, these babies have become fully formed individuals precisely because they are not attached to their biological parents, or to anyone in particular. Like Athena springing fully formed from the head of Zeus, a complete self and ready for action; someone to be reckoned with. I can't wait to meet them.

We look around, left to right, but the lobby is nearly deserted, no babies to be seen. Sheila gives us our keys and tells us to go on to our rooms; the babies will be brought there when they arrive.

The tension is palpable as we ride the elevator to our floor, tight looks on all the parents' faces. The only one who smiles for me, the only one who seems to share my excitement, is Maggie, and she mugs as I snap photos of her just before she is to meet her new sister. The elevator reaches our floor and the doors open.

"Well, here we go!" says Louise, as Maggie pulls her from the elevator. Jimmy is still grumbling about the schedule change. "Goddamn it, we don't even have anything unpacked!" he says as he exits, to no one in particular.

Each of the three families has a room along the same hallway on the fourth floor, and the other two couples disappear inside theirs. We find ours, the bags are brought by the porter, and Alex nervously begins to unpack the baby supplies she has brought with her. She is talking to herself, "Where did I put the diapers? I can't find the formula. . . ."

I can't stand it; I open the door and lean out into the corridor, trying to get a glimpse. Within moments I hear the elevator bell clang, and then a group of people steps off holding three babies, and my eyes lock upon the smallest little face, a baby, wrapped in a bulky padded suit with a hood covering her head, being carried down the hallway. I know instantly that this is the baby, the baby from the photograph. I don't even look at the others, though they are right behind in the arms of two other orphanage workers. Her face . . . I can't take my eyes off of her, there is something hauntingly familiar, and yet so strange about her. For one thing, she has the smallest nose I have ever seen. I can't tell, in this first moment, if she is beautiful or ugly. It is an unusual face, and I like it so much, it is so right and belongs to no other. She has big round eyes that hold the very serious expression of an old soul. It is just as I imagined: a complete self, not merely a "baby," worthy of respect surely, and perhaps more. What I am feeling in this moment is akin to awe; this person who has been rejected and abandoned being carried down the hallway, toward a fate she cannot guess, toward people she does not know, maintaining an expression so serene it is as if she were expecting to be crowned queen.

I hurry back inside the room and tell Alex that they are here, the baby is here. "You're kidding," she says, as if surprised.

"No, I'm not kidding," I answer, and go back outside into the hallway, the door closing behind me. I have my camera so that I can record this moment when Alex first meets her baby.

A man and two women, each holding a baby, stand at the doorway. Alex opens the door, and the man reads her last name from a sheet of paper he holds in his hand.

"Yes," she says, "that's me."

One of the women hands her the baby, the baby I knew was hers, and the three walk away, leaving this child we have never met before forever in our care. Alex stands holding the baby in the doorway with an expression I can't read. She is not smiling, and she very slowly reaches up and pulls the hood back from the baby's head to reveal sparse black hair underneath. The two just look at each other, for several long moments, neither one flinching, a Mexican standoff. And then the baby starts to cry, to express the self within her, to say "No, this is not what I want."

Alex turns with the baby and I follow her inside the room and close the door. The baby is crying very hard now, her face red, her mouth opened in a circle of fear. Alex halfheartedly bounces the baby up and down on her hip, saying, "Shh, shh," while I stand and stare at them; the attempts to calm her are ineffective, and the baby keeps crying.

Fear. I had not been expecting fear. But now I know I should have, this baby has never seen us or anyone who looks like us in her life. We must look like aliens to her, with our big noses and round eyes and not-black hair. This is so obvious to me now, and I am sobered by her reaction, and by my own lack of sensitivity to this possibility.

Alex sits down in a chair and lays the baby across her lap. The baby is struggling, trying to get away, and almost rolls off her lap. Alex tries to stick the nipple of a bottle into the baby's mouth but she turns her head violently, refusing it. Alex puts the bottle down and slides to the floor, and plops the baby onto her lap. She reaches for a colorful toy, and shakes it in front of the baby's red face, trying to distract her, but the baby ignores it and cries harder. Alex stands up and hands her to me, and I jiggle her up and down and sway side to side, saying, "It's okay, it's okay!" but the baby does not calm down.

Alex lays her on the bed and begins removing the heavy

padded suit. It is dirty, and it smells musty. Underneath, the baby wears a bright green cotton sweater and heavy pull-on pants. She is still crying as Alex removes each article and throws them in a heap next to the bed. As each layer comes off, it becomes increasingly clear how small this baby is, how tiny. Alex takes off the baby's T-shirt, and we look at her in silence as she lies on the bed in a diaper. She is so skinny, her arms and legs spindly and undeveloped.

"Oh my God," Alex says. "This baby can't be the age they said!" The agency told her the baby she was matched with was thirteen months old, but Alex is right, she does look only about the size of a seven- or eight-month-old. Alex begins looking her over, takes off her diaper, turns her onto her stomach. She smells; a close damp odor rises from the bed. Across her shoulders and back is a red rash, and tiny scars. "What is this?" Alex asks, to no one in particular. Certainly, I don't know, but to see a baby in this condition makes me feel sick. I am used to big, robust American babies, and this is a shock. Alex seems stunned, murmuring "oh," or "God," or "no," under her breath.

The baby lies quietly on the bed in front of us, not crying now, and looks back at us with an expression of grief and resignation. Neither Alex nor I say a word. I am thinking, Oh Jesus, oh Jesus, there is real sadness in this world, and it is represented here in this room by this child. This is no blithe adventure, and the excitement I felt just moments ago seems callow now in the face of this reality. Time stops as the three of us attempt to absorb our new realities, to find a way to accept that from now on nothing will be as we thought it would be.

In the transparency of this moment, Alex's feelings vibrate across our silence. They do not feel like love, or compassion. They feel like disgust, and I can sense her judgment of this child as she fails to reach out to touch or comfort her, the naked vulnerable child upon the bed.

What happens when one is suddenly confronted with the sick, the neglected, the dirty? Either the heart opens, or it slams shut against the assault. Is this a choice, or a reaction born of a million prior choices?

What happens when love does not come?

What happens when it does, so unexpectedly that it takes your breath away, and leaves you with a heart that aches, and longs for justice?

ॐ

Alex is in the room on the phone with her husband, telling him about the baby, and I am trying to induce the baby into sleep by walking with her, by singing to her, by murmuring words she cannot understand. We finally succeeded in feeding her bits of ham and vegetables from the room service meal we'd ordered. The baby was sitting in front of us in a stroller as we ate, and Alex held out a piece of food, just to see if she would take it. The baby literally lunged for the food, gobbling piece after piece until there was nothing left to give her. We looked at each other in horror, wondering, How starved is this child? "I just cannot *believe* this," Alex said.

After she ate, we bathed her, and the terrified crying that we had managed to stop began anew. It took both of us to hold her in the tub, each of us trying to quickly soap the slippery, wriggling body and rinse her so that the ordeal could end. When I pulled her from the tub, the water was dirty brown, and I noticed the grime still embedded under her fingernails. She clung to me, water dripping from her body, as if she were clinging to a piece of driftwood in a raging sea.

But now I hold her and she is quiet as we walk and walk. On one lap around the hotel's fourth floor, I see Curtis walking with his new baby, and I stop to look at her. Their baby is beautiful, and seems calm and alert. Jasmine, he tells me they have named her; and Jasmine, too, has an air of total self-possession about her. "Did she cry when you first got her?" I ask him, and he says no. "I'm not sure she's going to sleep, though!" he adds with a weary smile in which his pride is evident, and off he goes for another lap.

Finally the baby falls asleep in my arms, and I keep walking, thinking about her. Who is she? Who are her parents? Why was she given up? What woman bore this child through intense pain, only to relinquish her to the unknown? It is all a mystery, as if this baby had just dropped from the sky. No identity, no story, except the vague details that the orphanage wrote on her information sheet: found at a train station on New Year's Eve. No note or any evidence of her family's identity among her belongings, which consisted of only the clothes she wore that night as she fell asleep, not suspecting that when she awoke, there would be no one there, and she would be in a strange and frightening place, alone in the world. How many times is this scenario repeated, how many children left in the cold each day in China, I wonder.

"I'm so sorry, so sorry, little one," I say, over and over again. As I think of this, how scared she must have been, how desperate the cries in that cold empty station, a lump rises in my throat that I cannot swallow. I look down at the sweet face, so calm now, and I think, How could they, how could anyone . . . ? Was it desperation, or cruelty? And I think that already, after knowing her for only a few hours, I could not, no matter what, set her down and walk away; I could not leave her to an uncertain fate.

After we bathed her, Alex dressed her in a pink sleeper outfit that was way too big for her, and then propped her up on the bed with some pillows. The effect was pathetic, the too-big clothes swallowing her up, the propped-up little body in an awkward position. I wanted to move her, but Alex just stood, looking at her without saying anything. Finally, she broke the silence. "Do you think she's pretty?" she asked.

The baby looked back at us with an expression of the deepest sadness, a mixture of fear, grief, and incomprehension. I couldn't speak for a moment. What was there to say? Was she pretty? How could this possibly matter at this moment? Alex was judging her, this helpless sad baby, and I could tell by the question that she had already found her wanting.

I wanted to protect her, to shield her from this unfair and cruel judgment, and I answered yes; yes I think she's pretty. Yes, I think she may be the most beautiful baby I have ever seen. The relief on Alex's face was evident; the baby she was going to take was pretty, thank goodness. It was obvious that this was important to her, as important as anything else.

It was then that I picked up the baby, and offered to take her into the hallway so that Alex could call her husband; but what I really wanted was to hold the baby close, and whisper some comfort to her as she fell asleep tonight, so that she would know there was reason to hope. "Oh, baby, don't worry; you've come so far, it will be all right," I say to her, hoping it is true.

We walk around and around, until I see Alex poke her head out the doorway and motion for me to come in, she is off the phone. Back in the room, I place the sleeping baby into the small iron crib the hotel has provided. There are twin beds in the room, and Alex has unpacked some of her things and placed them on the bed farthest from the crib. "Here," I say, "you take this bed; you'll want to be close to the baby during the night."

"No, no," Alex says hastily. "This is fine, I'll sleep over here." She climbs into the bed, leaving me to the one next to the baby. In fact, the crib is pushed right up against my bed, so close that I can reach through the bars and touch her without having to get up. I don't mind, there is a little surge of pleasure at the thought of sleeping next to her on her first night away from the orphanage, though I wonder why Alex wouldn't want that pleasure for herself.

I put on my pajamas and get into bed. A little light is coming through the pulled curtains, and I can see the baby lying curled into a ball near the end of the crib. I fall asleep to the sound of her breathing, even and deep. When I awake some hours later, after fretful, brightly colored dreams, the first thing I see is the little face, peering at me in the half dark through the iron bars of the crib. For the briefest moment, in that twilight before fully awakening, when I have not yet remembered where we are, or why we are here, I feel as if I am looking into a face I have always known, always dreamed of, or always wished for. And the first thought that swims up from the depths of dream time: *my baby.*

∽

When I wake fully a little later and open my eyes, the baby is already awake, and looking at me through the bars of her crib, not making a sound of need or desire. I lean forward and poke my finger through the bars.

"Hello there, baby, how did you sleep?" I say.

Alex is just waking too, and she gets out of bed and comes

over to pull the baby from her crib. Today the parents are scheduled to complete adoption paperwork in a regional office not far from our hotel, and Alex is uptight about it. She is thinking, Will I have the right papers, what about the money? She seems far more focused on the administrative issues than on the baby, but I reason that this makes sense. If there is some glitch in the paperwork, the adoption could be in jeopardy.

Alex asks me to help with the baby; she hands her to me and I begin to dress her and get a bottle ready. She is quiet this morning, and lets me attend to her without any sort of struggle or fuss. When I put her down on the bed, she is unable to turn over; after being left lying in a crib for months on end in the orphanage, she does not have the strength.

The baby watches me intently, never taking her eyes from me. I talk to her. "So guess where we're going? You get to ride in your brand-new stroller!" I know she can't understand me, but think that it might be reassuring to her that I am trying. Alex walks by a few times, but doesn't interact with the baby, her mind caught up in the details of the paperwork.

There will be no time to write in my journal this morning, and I don't really mind, though the dream I had last night keeps entering my mind. It was odd, something about a woman, someone who was teaching me? I try to focus, and bring the images from the dream into my conscious mind: a woman . . . I can see her, she is standing before me; it seems she is Chinese. She is tall and beautiful, with glossy black hair reaching almost to the floor. She is telling me something about an emperor, that she has been sent to prepare me for marriage to him, and to bear his child, a child of our divine union. And then her words come back to me, and the details of the dream conversation unfold in my mind:

I asked Madam, "And why was it that I was chosen by the Emperor for this task? Does he not have many women in his court and many others in his lands who could provide him with a child?" I had seen them there, and I knew that many women visited his royal bedchambers in the night.

"Yes, it is true that the Emperor has many women from which to choose. But as with any other skill, only certain individuals have the spirit necessary to carry it to its highest levels. To master the teachings, one must be highly intelligent, of course; but she also must possess a fire within her, an unmistakable spark of the divine flowing from herself to others. It is this spark that the Emperor felt the day he saw you in the fields, and from this he knew that he must place you as the jewel in his crown."

"And what is he like, the Emperor?" I asked her.

After a silence, she answered, "He is very smart."

"Do you mean wise?" I asked.

"Wise? No, I cannot say wise. Wisdom is of the heart, and the Emperor has as yet to open his heart to wisdom. But as Empress you may help him in this. And you may be successful, so long as he does not know what you are doing," she answered, a mysterious tone in her voice.

I absorbed her words, and was quiet for a time. When I felt that I had begun to grasp her meaning, I began tentatively to formulate my thoughts.

"In my heart, I know that many suffer. In my own village, there are people without enough food, or who have no roof over their heads when the harvest is meager. If the Emperor could feel and know of their plight, perhaps he could send food from the vast imperial stores, or jewels from the treasure lining these walls. Is this what you mean?" I asked. Madam looked at me for a long moment. She had an expression that I could not read,

*and I thought, for just an instant, that I saw something like re-
lief in her eyes.*

*"Exactly this," she said slowly. "China is a vast land, a land
of uncounted souls. If your little village suffers thus, imagine
that suffering played out across this great countryside! And
imagine what an Emperor of compassion could do to help those
suffering souls. You have been placed in a unique position, an
opportunity that not many receive in this life. You, through
your position, have the power to change an untold number of
lives. And what will you choose to do with this opportunity? It
is up to you."*

*I inhaled her words. They came to me like a fragrance, the
bracing scent of juniper, the sweet smell of lilies, the glory of
truth revealed, which has no form. I closed my eyes and envi-
sioned those souls, and for a moment I was hovering above
them in a robe of fiery red and gold, on the back of a dragon
breathing fire. They reached up their arms to me; they reached
up their arms. . . .*

They reached up their arms. . . . The intensity of the dream images leaves me rooted to the spot in the middle of the room
until Alex comes by and says, "Hey, where are you?" and I shake
my head and laugh a little, coming out of my reverie. Now that
the baby is with us, things will be different. I can see already
that Alex will want me to be far more involved in the care of the
baby than I thought.

There is a knock on our door and Alex goes to open it. It is
Anna, and she has some papers for Alex. They stand at the door
conferring about something, and then Alex comes back inside
and tells me she must run downstairs, to the business office in

the hotel. There is an important document that she needs to have faxed to her, can I watch the baby? She is now even more nervous and begins searching through her briefcase, mumbling something about the adoption agency "screwing up."

"Of course," I tell her, and go to warm a bottle. Alex leaves and I pick up the baby and take her to the chair in the corner of the room. When I offer the bottle she takes it easily, looking up at me, her eyes wide open as she sucks hard on the nipple. Finally getting some nourishment, finally being touched and held . . . it has already made a difference in these few short hours since we got her. She seems brighter, more alert, not so listless. Already not the same baby; already beginning to bloom into what she can become. I look at her and think, How amazing . . . the resilience of the human spirit.

"You amaze me, baby!" I say, and in her eyes I see something new: trust.

ura

When we meet the other two couples in the lobby, it is obvious that the night for them was long and sleepless. Curtis and Judy have dark circles under their eyes; Jasmine hardly slept. Louise and Jimmy tell us they were up circling the hallway most of the night with their little one. Jimmy proudly shows us their new baby, whom he is holding in his arms. She, too, is adorable, and has enough hair that they have made a little ponytail that shoots straight up from her head.

"Our baby slept!" I tell them, and they murmur envious approval. Even though they had a difficult night, they already seem like families, and we are not. It is incredible how after a few short hours, these babies look exactly right in the arms of their new parents. This morning I am acutely aware that Alex, the baby, and I are not a family, and I feel a twinge of doubt about my presence here. Anna tells us it is time to go, and I push the baby stroller toward the door.

We board a van outside the hotel and drive a short distance into the city. We get out and walk a few blocks down busy streets, a strange processional, three Caucasian women carrying bundles from which emerge three tiny Chinese faces. Many people stop to gawk or poke a companion and point our way. I am carrying the baby, as Alex is carrying the bulging, heavy briefcase that contains the vital adoption paperwork, as well as a sum in cash to be handed over to officials before the adoption can proceed.

The money has to be in new, fresh, unmarked bills—three thousand dollars. Alex was instructed to bring only twenty-dollar bills, with no stray marks or creases evident anywhere on them, or the adoption could be refused. We joked about this before the trip, how it made the whole exchange feel clandestine, like an undercover drug deal, or a payoff to the mob. The Chinese government insisted on thousands of dollars for a baby that someone had literally thrown away. What, or whom, was that money for, exactly?

We enter a cold, dark concrete building and climb the stairs to the third floor, where we come to a large room filled with people, all adopting Chinese babies. Some speak French, they are Canadians; and there are a few from a Scandinavian country. But for the most part the adoptive parents are American. Alex goes off to check over the paperwork before she is called for the appointment, and I rock the baby and sing to her, give her a bottle, and watch as the new families are born. After the meeting with a government official behind closed doors, the parents emerge looking relieved and happy, and are taken to a corner of the room where their pictures are taken with their new babies. The babies are all so cute, and they all look so different, some chubby, some skinny, some with lots of hair and some with none.

It is a long time before a Chinese official comes to the doorway and announces Alex's name in a loud voice. Alex motions for me to come over, and bring the baby. I move to hand the baby to her, but she says, "No, you come in too, and hold her while I take care of the business." She seems nervous.

"Are you sure?" I ask, vaguely uncomfortable. I wonder if it's even allowed, the Chinese officials are so prickly about following procedure to the letter.

"Of course," she says. "I can't do this by myself."

We enter a small office, empty except for a spare metal desk and chair, the bare window allowing the bright winter sunlight to shine in on the dust and grime. An imposing middle-aged Chinese man in military uniform is sitting behind the desk; he does not look up or acknowledge us when we sit in the metal chairs before him. There is silence as he rifles through the stack of papers. After some time he begins to speak. Anna is there to act as translator, and she poses the questions to Alex:

"What is your family income?"

Alex hesitates a moment, and then states a figure in the hundreds of thousands of dollars.

Now I am really uncomfortable, and I can tell she is too, though she doesn't look at me, and is trying to hide her discomfort. Her mouth is set in a hard line. I wonder what the man thinks, this must sound like a fortune; most people in China live on less than a dollar a day. But he doesn't skip a beat. The man goes on:

"What kind of house do you live in?" he asks in his guttural Chinese. Anna translates.

Alex answers, telling him about their lovely house, the bedroom designated for the baby, the nice, safe neighborhood.

"Are there other children in the household?" he asks through Anna.

"I have a son who is eight years old," she replies.

"Who will stay home with the child?" he asks.

"I will," she says.

I know this to be untrue. Alex has told me for months that she plans to continue working and that the baby will be placed in day care five days a week, from the very beginning. I wonder why she doesn't tell the truth, and then I think that maybe the adoption agency told her to lie, that it might jeopardize the adoption.

"What type of work do you and your husband do?" the man asks.

"I am in medical sales," she says, "and my husband has a consulting business."

"What is your education?"

"I have a master's degree," she answers. She is sitting stiffly, hands folded in her lap, and I can tell she is trying to just get through this.

I sit holding the baby, listening to this string of concerned questions, and it makes me want to laugh. It seems odd, to be so fastidiously checking the backgrounds and resources of these people who have come from halfway around the world to adopt children that no one in China seems to want, or be able to care for. The man is very stern, as if lecturing wayward schoolchildren.

And then he asks his last question: "Do you promise to never abandon this child?"

The question hangs in the air as I think of the audacity of this inquiry from a representative of a government whose own policies have caused the problem of abandoned babies in the first place. This is like a show, an elaborate stage play that we are supposed to believe is real. We are supposed to believe that they really care for these babies, when millions are cast aside. The government has been trying to control raging population growth with the draconian one-child policy; but don't they know their own people, their own cultural biases? It seems like a willful disregard of truth, of reality. The bias toward male children here is an ancient cultural artifact; to ignore its power over people's choices has produced this disaster, has produced this orphaned child in my arms.

I kiss the top of the baby's head, so warm and soft, just as Alex answers the question, "No, never."

〜

We return to the hotel, and I decide to go to the gym for a while. When I get back to the room, it is late afternoon, and Alex already has the baby in her sleeper for the night. She is going about her business, folding some baby clothes and laying them out on the bed while the baby plays quietly on the floor.

"I'm so exhausted," Alex says, a hint of despair in her voice.

"Yes, of course you're exhausted," I say, trying to reassure her. "Anyone would be, such a grueling trip, and caring for the baby. . . . Why don't we order some food?"

"I'm not hungry," she answers.

"Well, I think I will, though; are you sure you don't want anything?" I ask.

Alex speaks in a flat, hard tone. "I can't do this." She continues folding the clothes, not looking up.

I continue doing what I'm doing, taking off my running shoes, finding some clothes to change into; I sit down on the chair in the corner across the room. It takes me some moments to understand what she has said, to begin to know that nothing will ever be the same. I look down at the baby, she is trying to fit a plastic shape into its hole on the toy she is playing with. Her little body lists forward toward the toy. She is unable to sit up straight, her spine still weak, the muscles unused, and yet she is trying so hard to keep herself upright, so she can play with the toy, something new, something interesting. I feel a little spasm in my heart, a twinge of physical pain as I see the little bit of happiness this toy is giving her, and that it might soon be taken away.

Something in the frigid tone of Alex's voice frightens me. I feel suddenly very cold all over; the beginnings of physical shock. What could she mean, I ask myself. But I know what she means. To clarify, to buy time, to make her say it, I ask, "Can't do this? What do you mean?"

"I can't take this baby," she says.

This cannot possibly be. Take it back, I think; now that you've heard yourself say it, I will give you a chance to back yourself out of this. "Do you mean you can't take care of her now? Because I can help you, if—if that's what you need," I stammer.

"No," she says firmly. "I mean, I don't think I can take her at all. I can't take her home," she says so resolutely I know she means it. She can't take her, can't give this child a home. She can't save her; she can't save herself.

"But . . . but you have to, don't you? I mean, what else would you do?" I ask. My mind whirls, trying to figure out where I stand now in this strange incomprehensible new landscape, this inhospitable country of rejection. I just don't understand this, what is she saying?

"I'm going to turn her back in, send her back to the orphanage," she says. She has this all figured out, she has decided. She says it as if she is returning a blouse to a department store, no more or less of an emotional investment than that. A mundane transaction, an inconvenience, something to be taken care of; the tone of her voice chills me again, and suddenly a passionate need to stop this from happening takes hold.

"No. *No!*" I almost shout. "Don't do that! You can't do that." She looks at me evenly, and I realize that she can do that, and she will do that, unless I can convince her otherwise. "I'll help you; I can take care of her for the rest of the trip, until you get home and you're feeling better. You're just tired and over-whelmed, you need some rest. . . ."

"I don't want to take her home," she says, her voice flat and unyielding. She turns from me and continues folding the clothes, the little baby clothes that she will no longer need. I do not know this person; this is the part of herself she has kept from me. I have never known the person who is capable of this coldness.

"But . . . why?" I ask. "Why can't you take her?" My voice rises in disbelief. "What's wrong with her? She's perfect!" And I realize at that moment that to me she is exactly that: perfect. I look over at her and see the innocence and beauty shining forth, and I want to grab her, to run from this place.

Alex continues. "It's just not what I expected; I don't feel how I expected to feel. It doesn't feel right," she explains. It explains nothing. It is all about her; not one word of concern for the baby.

"But, I mean . . . so what?" I say, with a hollow little laugh. "You made a commitment; you can't back out of something like this now! You've got to think this through; you can't make a decision like this tonight, you've got to give this some time." I think of the trauma this baby has been through already, in being taken from the orphanage and getting used to us, and now to send her back? What would that do to her? "I can help you. . . . I would even take the baby for a while after we get home, just until you're feeling better."

"But," she says, "what if I take her home and I don't feel better? I can't take that risk. I can't put my family through something like that."

"Have you talked with your husband about this? Have you made this decision alone?" I ask.

"He didn't really want the adoption in the first place; it was my decision. But I can't do this if he's not supportive. . . . I just can't do this!"

"What can't you do? You wanted a child . . . right?" I ask. She never told me of her husband's hesitation, never once mentioned he might not want to adopt.

"I wanted a child, not an infant! This baby is NOT thirteen months old! The adoption agency lied to me, the Chinese government lied to me, and I don't want a child this young!"

"But Alex . . . look; I mean, she'll grow up!" I say, stating the obvious. "It won't be long before she'll seem like a thirteen-month-old! She's behind in development but she won't always be." I am thinking, She is going to give this child back over a difference of five months?

And then she wails, her voice rising like a petulant child, "I don't *want* to go to Gymboree!" For a second I am disoriented, I have no idea what she is talking about.

"What? What is Gymboree?" I ask, truly confused.

She tells me about how she took her son to Gymboree when he was young, where they play games and sing songs together. If she has a child this young, she will have to take her to Gymboree. Though I don't know anything about Gymboree, what I gather she is saying is that she doesn't want to put the time into developing this child.

"Gymboree . . . it's not mandatory, is it? I mean, you don't have to go by some law or something?" I ask.

"Of course not!" she barks, as if she is explaining to an idiot. "But *everyone does it!*"

I realize at this point it makes no sense to pursue the conversation in this way; she is becoming more and more agitated, and rationality seems to be waning. More than a year spent planning for this adoption, and less than twenty-four hours after she gets the baby, she wants to back out? I can't grasp what is happening, it is unbelievable. Alex is the last person I would have thought would do this; she has always seemed ultra-responsible, not flighty in the least. It makes no sense, no sense at all, and I rationalize that she just needs some time and space, and she will snap out of this.

I feel no hesitation in saying, "If you get home and still don't want to keep her, I'll take her."

There is no choice; how else to buy time? Alex looks at me intently, and immediately takes me up on it.

"You would?" She stops moving around the room, and puts her hands on her hips. "You would take her?" she asks. Her tone is hopeful, her demeanor anticipatory.

I take a moment, and draw a deep breath.

"Yes. Yes," I say, "I would."

I want Alex to feel that she has some options, to not feel so much pressure to give the baby back right away. But I also know that it is true: I would take her, I would not hesitate in doing so. I believe Alex's mood is a passing thing, Alex will be over it in a day or two, and we will go about our lives the way we had planned; but if it is not a passing thing, I am prepared to stand by my offer.

"I'll take the baby out. Why don't you call your husband and talk this over with him?" I suggest, thinking that he will try to talk her out of abandoning the baby. She agrees and I pick up the baby, grateful that she can't understand a word we are saying.

I am shaking as I hold the baby, walking around and around the hallway again. For well over an hour we walk and I talk to her, tell her it's going to be all right, and she falls asleep in my arms. I sit down on the floor with my back against the wall and hold her, sick to my stomach, feeling light-headed. Suddenly, nothing in the world makes sense. This is the baby that was going to be my godchild; Alex asked me to be her godmother the week before we left: it was an acknowledgment of the importance of the role I will play on this trip, and I took it seriously, maybe more seriously than Alex did. It was a commitment to watch out for this child in a spiritual sense, to do what I could to keep her soul from harm, to protect her.

I was going to be part of her life, and I was excited about that, and now it is all in jeopardy. Last night I bathed her, fed her, rocked her to sleep, and all day today I held her and kept her close. She already smiled at me, this morning when I changed her diaper, after we made it through that first horrible night. It seems like it might be the first smile she has ever smiled; I could see her watching me, mimicking me as she tried hard to pull the corners of her mouth into a grin to mirror mine. And when I bent to kiss her with tender affection, the look of surprise on her face made me certain she had rarely, if ever, been kissed.

And I had dreams about her, several dreams about a dark-eyed baby, months before I even saw her. A dark-eyed baby, my terrible dream of forgetting, could that have been her? Weren't we connected, already, in some intimate way? How could I now just leave her behind, as if she had never been?

The terrible dream . . . a year ago, when I spent a month alone in a rented cottage near the beach a few hours' drive from my home—I was at a turning point and needed a break, and wanted to spend some time writing, thinking, getting clear on what I was supposed to do with my life. Looking in the want ad section of our local paper, I noticed an advertisement for a beach house in a small town a couple of hours away. I called the number listed in the ad and spoke with an older lady, who owned the house. After I explained to her that I was looking for a place to retreat, she paused a moment, and then said, "I think this was meant to be. It has been a magical place for me. . . . You'll love it, and it's just big enough for one person!" It sounded perfect, and sight unseen, I rented the house for a month.

The first few days, I was terrified, angry, amused, bored, and most of all, lonely. It was a loneliness that attached to no specific person; it was the loneliness of one who has been, for a long time, disconnected from themselves. Meditation became a refuge. I would sit for hours, in lotus position, my back pressed against the couch, trying to clear and focus my mind. Several times, I experienced a strange disorientation, and had the feeling that my body no longer existed, that I was no longer connected to the world. And more than once, I was aware of a presence in the room, and though I could not see a form, I could sense movement, and a frisson of energy that emanated from something. I had nowhere to go, nothing to do, no distractions to pull me away once I began.

Days began blending into nights. I started sleeping at odd hours, and waking in the middle of the night. Sometimes I would wake from a dream that felt so real that it took several minutes to reorient myself. These dreams all seemed connected in some way, with recurrent characters, locations, and themes, though I could not always remember the entire dream when I awoke. Each morning I would start the day sitting on the front porch with a strong cup of coffee and my journal, recording the dreams of the night before. Very often, that was the only writing that got accomplished that day.

One night I had a dream that was so disturbing that I awoke from it choking on my tears. I dreamed that I had suddenly, inexplicably remembered that I had a baby. Somewhere there was a baby that I had given birth to and then placed aside, forgotten, neglected. It was not a deliberate act of neglect; my mind had betrayed me, had suffered a complete erasure of memory. Until that moment in the dream when the knowing came with a shock, I had been living in complete ignorance of her existence. Now that I remembered, the utter horror and shame of forgetting made me question whether or not I deserved to live.

My dream self thought, Where is she? Where did I last put her down? All I knew was that it had been too long . . . too long for a baby to go without care, to be without love. I moved in the agonizing slow-motion way of dreams down a long hallway toward where I thought she might be, and in the weird perfect logic of the dream world, it happened to be the room in which my mother had died, in the house where I grew up.

I entered the room, which was darkened and had a closed-up feeling. There in the corner next to the window was a crib, and I knew that my baby was inside it. This is where I had left her, and the cold dread of what I might find was too much to bear. If she was dead, if I had not found her in time, my life was over too; I could not live with the knowledge that I had been responsible for my own baby's death. The crib loomed up before me; it was all I could see. I looked down and there she was, my child, and I knew instantly and with a wave of gratitude that she was still alive, that I had found her just in time.

She was barely breathing as I lifted her from the crib and looked into her face. Her eyes were huge and dark and luminous, and they held no recrimination for me. The eyes reflected that the soul behind them was at peace, and in that peace I saw my own salvation. I put my finger to her lips and she began sucking, hard, and with each pull she grew stronger and stronger until she was a robust glowing baby, alive in my arms.

I could not shake the dream for days. The feeling that I had been expiated from some guilt that I could not name permeated my waking life. I recorded the dream in my journal just as I had the others; and for the next five days and nights, no more dreams came, and no more writing; until the last night of my stay in the tiny house, when dreaming and waking merged, leaving me awed, and wondering.

❧

Alex comes to the doorway and motions for me to come inside. She says she is feeling better; her husband calmed her down and helped her think through the situation. My relief must be apparent; she smiles at me and gives the baby a little pat as we walk into the room. Her husband has asked to speak to me, would I talk to him? He is still on the phone.

I put the baby, still sound asleep, down in her crib. I pick up the phone receiver, my hand shaking. "What in the heck happened?" he says, incredulous. I tell him that I'm not sure, not sure at all yet. I tell him that she is exhausted and needs some rest, and agree when he asks me if I will make sure she gets some sleep and that she keeps eating. I tell him I will take care of the baby; I'll do anything to help. And when he asks, "How's the baby?" my voice breaks as I answer, "She's beautiful."

His tone is worried and subdued. I can tell he knows this is not just a passing thing. He confirms what Alex said, that he never really wanted to adopt; Alex talked him into it. Actually, he tells me that she threatened him when he would not agree; threatened to leave him and take their son, and he was afraid she might do it. "And now this," he says. It is not the time for me to say, How could you allow this? It is not the time to say, This is insanity. I say, "What do we do now?" and he answers, "Just get everyone home."

"I'm glad you're there with her," he says before we hang up. I think but I don't say, It should be you here, instead of me.

Alex and I then talk far into the night. I slip into my familiar therapist mode, mostly listening as she spills out her fears and doubts; she tells me things about her childhood and her relationship with her mother, about why she thought she wanted a child. She wanted, she says, for someone to love her again, the way her son does, the way only a child can. The classic wrong reason, the worst reason in the world to have a child, so that he or she can love you.

She keeps saying that the baby is too young, she cannot care for an infant, the agency told her the baby was thirteen months old, a toddler. To me, the baby looks and acts like a thirteen-month-old who has been neglected; it is as if we are experiencing two different babies. Besides, I think, anyone adopting from China knows that sometimes you do not get the individual baby that has been promised to you; you don't choose. It is part of the deal to accept that there will be unknowns. Alex wondered yesterday if the baby she was given was the same one from the photograph she received from the adoption agency. I told her I felt certain that it was, only because I recognized her in the hallway at first sight, and how else would I have been able to do so?

Alex tells me things I never knew. She tells me that she has never gotten along with her sister, that they were always vying for her mother's attention and approval. I can't see what all this has to do with this child; but it is clear to me that there are serious emotional and psychological issues from her past that have never been addressed, and for some reason they are all coming to a head in this moment. In clinical parlance it is called decompensation: a traumatic event or intense emotion becomes a catalyst for a psychic break.

In all the years we have known each other, we have never talked like this. I cannot remember a time when she betrayed strong emotions; she has always been of a controlled nature. But now, her pain is obvious: she truly does not understand her feelings, or what has happened. She is crying and reaching out to me, but I cannot be fully sympathetic because of the little baby sleeping a few feet away in the crib. That child is innocent, and totally vulnerable to Alex's feelings of confusion; should not at least one adult put this baby's needs first, above their own?

Alex is crying for herself, not for the baby, and my heart

sinks further as the tangled web of her psyche weaves before me. I try hard to fit what Alex is saying into various psychological theories, but the pieces do not fit together in any sort of rational way. Clinically, there is no designation for it, but what I am witnessing here seems to be something like a classic nervous breakdown.

I am on the edge of an abyss, with no choice but to step off that edge, into the unknown, beyond psychology, beyond rationality, beyond the easily explainable. A child's life is at stake, as well as the long-term emotional well-being of my friend; if she leaves the baby here, would she ever be able to forgive herself? There is no question of this being my responsibility. I am here now, I agreed to come; and now the only question is, what can I do to assist in bringing about the best outcome? Because I already know the answer to the question: Would I be able to forgive myself if I did not?

When she has finally talked and cried herself out, we try to sleep. I lie there in the dark, thinking about the baby, wanting to cry myself. Tomorrow we are scheduled to visit the orphanage, which is an unusual privilege; not all adoptive parents get to see the institutions that have housed their children, but somehow we have been given permission to visit the Jiujiang Children's Welfare Institute. Surely after we go there, Alex won't be able to give her back. One more day of bonding, of getting to know this child; each hour that goes by will make it more and more inconceivable for her to relinquish her baby.

"Her baby." It is then that I realize, Alex has never once called her by the name she chose for her. Not once. We have both been calling her "the baby." I did not notice until now this lack of desire to claim her, to humanize her by giving her a name.

Whose baby was she, whose would she be? Who would name her, love her, hold her, dry her tears?

I would, Baby, if I could. And as I fall into restless sleep, Baby's face swims before me, tears like glistening pearls running down her cheeks, and as I drift into a dream of lost happiness, I hear her calling, calling for her mother, the mother she has lost.

Love

I had entered another series of courtyards, open to the sky, surrounded by more chambers and high stone walls. I had not been in this place before, and I saw no one as I walked along, looking curiously into each courtyard, trying to appear casual in front of my guard, Jiang. I was looking for a man I had seen the day before, a man named Han. Where had he disappeared to, and what was this place? Just as this question came to mind, I passed the opening to a large, sunlit lawn, surrounded by stone walls, and in the center of the lawn stood Han, holding his sword in perfect position.

Han turned, and opened his eyes. This time, there was surprise in them, but the warrior did not flinch. He held his position for a moment, absorbing the new information of a change in his environment, and then his arm fell, dropping the sword.

He began striding across the lawn. Before Han even reached us, I began, "It was my doing. . . . I did not know my way, and came upon you here . . . please forgive us for disturbing your practice."

Han did not respond until he stood directly before me. Now that we stood so close I could see that his eyes held depth and kindness, and the hint of a smile played around them. "Mistress, I am relieved at the interruption for today. I had not the passion for my sword that one must have to complete the practice well," he said.

I returned his smile. "No passion for your sword? Yes, I see how this could be difficult for a warrior. But for a man, I should think this may be a relief. Am I correct?" I asked, looking Han directly in the eye.

Han looked back at me for a long moment, a sad expression suddenly coming and then going again, to be replaced by a quizzical look, which held there. "And, Mistress, how could you guess how a man might feel?" he asked softly, looking down, taking his eyes from mine.

I waited and did not respond. I waited for the right timing of my words. The swirling in my heart that had begun when I first saw Han grew stronger, and I released it into the gap between us; it was for him.

When it had reached him, I knew it, for he lifted his eyes to mine. In those eyes was a look so stark and naked, a look of grief and pain such as I had not seen. And I said then, my voice gentle as a breeze, "That is what I should like to ask you, sir."

We stood looking at each other just as the last waves of chanting from the monks in the outer court drifted to heaven.

"Let us walk," he said, and we began that journey that two begin who know: we hold time, love, and beauty in our hands, and there shall be a time when all veils shall fall.

ↄ

So many dreams and impressions to record; last night, a dream of a man, someone to whom I felt deeply connected. He seemed familiar. Could it be the same man in all these dreams? He was a warrior, or soldier, and I spoke to him in a courtyard surrounded by high walls. Walls again, I muse; where China is concerned it seems there are always walls, keeping people out, keeping people in. Manipulating people and space, putting limitations on both; the idea of containing what is feared seems to have deep roots in the Chinese psyche.

Alex is holding the baby and I have taken out my notebook, but cannot begin to write. I want to try to recall more details, but I am paralyzed by my feelings since Alex told me she doesn't want the baby. I am just hoping, hoping that today she will come to her senses. I look at the baby, decked out in a white knit cap and pink fleece coat, so innocent, and not suspecting that her fate hangs in the balance.

Before we visit the orphanage, we first must stop at yet another government office to attend to official adoption business, to satisfy another layer of government regulation. We left early this morning, and have been riding in the van for at least an hour already. The orphanage is in a dusty town a hundred miles from Nanchang, in Jiangxi province, a poor and rural area dominated by rice fields and farmland. From the window of the van I see women tending rice paddies, and men driving oxen with plows. Much of this countryside looks to have been untouched by time or the modern world. The houses are low-slung and made of mud and thatch; the people farm much as their ancestors did hundreds of years ago.

I put my notebook away with a sigh, just as we arrive in front of a stark cinder-block building, on a busy street lined with people. A crowd gathers as we unload from the van, some in the back craning their necks to see us better. Judy says she has heard that sometimes parents of abandoned babies will gather here to look, to see if they can spot their child in the arms of an American couple.

The office of adoptions is on the second floor, and we climb the dark and dirty stairwell to reach it. We are shown to a sparsely furnished room, where we will wait until summoned, once again, by a government official. This meeting is more of a formality than the last; we are here only to pick up the official adoption papers that have already been processed. We wait, and I hold Baby, and I feel the tension start to release. Alex seems better today, less stressed; she is laughing a little with the others. Maybe the storm has already passed, and Baby is safe. By the time we meet with the officials, I am feeling almost giddy, and I even ask Anna to ask the burly man in a military uniform who stamps Baby's official papers if he likes his job. Anna speaks in Chinese to him, and a huge smile splits his face, and he nods vigorously. "Yes, yes," he says, "I like seeing the babies."

As we get back into the van for the short drive to the orphanage, I scan the crowd, which has grown larger since we have been inside the building. I don't know what I'm looking for, but I am holding Baby, and maybe I will notice some spark of interest or recognition from someone there, and I will know that there was someone who cared enough about Baby to stand and wait, in hopes of seeing her again. Maybe her mother is that young girl there, in the back, with the newborn slung across her chest; perhaps her grandmother is that one, standing just in front, with the dirty apron; or maybe her father waits in the shadows, trying to appear nonchalant, but with a heart aching from pretending that his daughter does not exist.

But I see nothing, no such spark of interest, and we climb into the van once again. To reach the orphanage, we turn off the main road and onto a pile of rubble. To call it a road would be too generous. It is at most a path of rock, mud, and gravel leading between the buildings, and the little van in which we are riding heaves and rocks and grinds its way along its length. We move slowly enough to make eye contact with people sitting on stoops, walking with large dirty bundles, or riding rickety bicycles along the perilous roadway. Dilapidated houses, made of concrete, or cinder blocks, or mud; it is hard to distinguish the materials, as everything—buildings, people, landscape, animals, sky—is bathed in shades of brown or gray. A small boy, glimpsed through a broken windowpane that is framed by rusty iron bars, watches solemnly and without expression as we pass his grim, darkened house. I look very closely; this is where Baby would have lived, or someplace much like it, had her parents kept her.

The van pulls onto a paved plaza after waiting several minutes for a group of thin, tired-looking men to pile enough stone onto the roadway so that we can pass. I can't tell if they are reconstructing or deconstructing the road, but their work has reduced it to a swath of mud that the small van would have had difficulty navigating if they had not added more stones. The workers watch us with severe, suspicious expressions as we step out of the vehicle and bundle the three Chinese babies into strollers and move toward the orphanage. There is silence among our group as we walk slowly in the chilly winter sunshine, toward what we fear seeing, and yet must see. All the parents agreed that it was important to know the conditions of the orphanage, no matter how unpleasant the experience might be. It took some doing for Anna to convince officials to allow the visit; but now, as we draw closer, I sense reluctance. The mood of the group is somber; even Maggie is quiet as we walk.

I am surprised to see ahead of us a shiny, high granite wall with large golden letters, in English, proclaiming LOVE IN THE WORLD and LIFE FOR CHILDREN. This wall must have been very expensive to build, and is so out of place here, where everything else looks to be in a state of collapse. Two days ago, I would have been sure this is cynical propaganda, built here at the entrance of the orphanage only to fool Americans who come to adopt. But I have observed here an intense need to be liked by us, a childlike desire to impress. Perhaps that's what this is, a sincere attempt to show their good faith where these children are concerned, that they are trying to do the right thing in an impossible situation.

The front of the orphanage is very well kept too, with a paved courtyard and no rubble around. I am beginning to think this is not so bad, not half as bad as I thought it would be, and then I step inside, out of the hazy sunshine, and into a dark corridor, where I stand waiting for my eyes to adjust to the gloom. As I stand here I become aware that it is much colder inside the building than outside. It is the kind of cold that seeps into your bones, and permeates your mind, making your senses sharp at first, and then numb as the freezing takes hold.

My first thought is that there could not possibly be babies in here, in this cold, but then I see them, just inside the doorway. At least ten babies are lined up in wooden seats along the corridor, all swaddled in mismatched layers of clothing, unmoving and silent, their eyes trained upon us as we stand uncertainly in the corridor. A staff member in a white coat comes to greet us, and ushers us into one of several dark rooms just off the hallway. Inside the first room, rows and rows of cribs are pushed up against one another, filled with what look like layers and layers of bedding. I walk along the rows and look more closely, and see that there are small dark heads inside each bed, newborns, infants, some sleeping and some awake, all silent, not a cry to be heard. In each crib one or two babies are kept—there must be somewhere close to forty babies in this room alone, with one staff person to care for them all.

The room has no natural light, and in the midday it is dark and cheerless. Concrete floors, tile walls, metal cribs, and dirty linens make up the harsh environment for the smallest, most vulnerable creatures I have ever seen. I peer into as many cribs as I can, trying to make eye contact, to send a silent message of futile and heartbreaking love, which comes upon me with such power that it is suddenly hard to breathe. My chest fills up, something hard rises into my throat . . . one of the babies keeps reaching for my hand, whirling her arms like a windmill, as if to propel herself forward and into my arms.

I lean over her, noting the downy softness of her spiky black hair, and see the hope that is visible in her keen, shining eyes.

She still believes, I think; still believes in the goodness of human beings. It would be so easy to just pick this child up, to carry her away from here and make a place for her in my life. It would be the natural thing to do. The unnatural thing is leaving her here, leaving any of these babies to their uncertain futures. Her child's mind must sense that if she could make it into someone's arms, it would be against nature to put her down again, and that is why she seems to be willing herself into mine.

"I'm sorry," I whisper to the unnamed child. "They would never let me leave with you. There's red tape, regulations, money to be exchanged . . . a process." How could she understand this lunacy, when I do not? I touch her cheek and move away, and from the corner of my eye I can see her still waving her little arms, not giving up, not giving in.

The visitors are allowed to view just three of the nursery rooms on the first floor of the orphanage, and the rooms are identical, with rows of cribs, an unrelenting chilliness, and unbroken silence. I ask Anna if she will translate some questions I have, and we approach one of the staff members, a middle-aged woman in a white coat, who is overseeing the babies in the corridor.

"How many babies are here?" I ask. Anna speaks my question in Chinese, and the woman responds.

"Three hundred babies come here each year," she replies through Anna.

"Three hundred?" I think about this. "How many of those get adopted?" I ask.

Again, Anna speaks to her and she responds.

"Maybe one third," comes the answer.

One third. If each year three hundred babies are brought here, and only one hundred of those ever leave, what happens to the rest? Where are they? Two hundred babies times just five years is one thousand children! I haven't seen or, even more tellingly, heard any evidence that there are a thousand children here.

Before I have even fully formulated the thought, the question pops out of my mouth.

"How many die?" I ask.

Anna hesitates, and looks at me for a moment before she poses the question to the woman in the white coat. Immediately the woman shakes her head, speaking harshly.

"She won't talk about that," says Anna.

"Well, what happens to the ones who live but are never adopted? Will she talk about that?" I ask, irritation in my voice.

Anna translates the response. "They live here, in the orphanage, are educated, and trained for some type of work."

It is clear that the woman is very uncomfortable with this line of questioning, and so is Anna. I am exhausted thinking of this. What could all this mean, what happens to these children? And this is just one orphanage in one small provincial town. China is a country of over a billion people. . . . I read somewhere that the UN estimates that over a million girl children are "missing" from the population each year; a million children that are abandoned, aborted, or killed outright, just for being female. When I read that statistic, it was just a number; now that I have seen real flesh and blood examples of the statistic, it becomes another matter entirely. My mind and heart feel oppressed by the magnitude of human suffering represented by that number and the question it gives birth to: what is to be done?

And the work these children are trained for, is that military service, or backbreaking factory labor? Perhaps they are left to end up falling into a life of prostitution, service in a brothel; there will certainly be a need for more of those as the skewed demographic gets worse and all these male children grow up

and have trouble finding wives. I think of the beautiful baby I
have just touched, she of the desperately waving arms. . . .

Now Alex hands Baby to me. Several times already during
our time here she has found a reason to give her over to me,
and at this moment Baby's warmth and weight is a comfort to
me, she is a symbol of hope, however small. Surely now that
Alex has seen this place, and what she would be sending her
back to, no question could remain about taking this child. To
give up the chance to bring one of these lost children home? I
can't conceive of it, and I rejoice for Baby even as I grieve for
those left behind.

Some strange, unexpected connection has been forged between me and these children. Though I have known Baby for
only a day and a half, she seems an intimate part of me. And the
babies I have seen so briefly in their cribs just now . . . I am sure
I will see their faces in my mind for the rest of my life. We cannot just slip in and out of each other's lives as easily as we assume.

Maybe it's the nature of this trip—the heightened emotional
atmosphere around the adoptions—or it could be the attention
you must give to things when you are outside your natural
habitat, things that would ordinarily go unnoticed. Whatever
has allowed me a glimpse into the true nature of our effect on
each other, I know now in my depths that each and every interaction, however brief, between two human beings leaves an in-
delible mark behind.

I take Baby into the room where she was housed for the first
year of her life. The staff worker in white takes her from me,
and Anna says that the woman was Baby's caretaker for most of
the time since she was brought here. Baby has been silent and
solemn, but content in my arms while I've carried her about

this place. But upon being picked up by the caretaker, she becomes visibly upset, her eyes dart to mine, questioning. The caretaker smiles sheepishly while the baby squirms in her arms. The woman puts her down in a crib and says, through Anna, that this is Baby's crib. Baby looks dejected, her sad eyes wide, her mouth drawn down at the corners. I can almost hear her thoughts. . . . Are you leaving me here? I reach down, unable to stand even a brief troubling of her heart. She puts her arms around my neck and I pull her from the tiny prison and walk away with her, out into the corridor.

Many of the babies are still here, in the unusual wooden chairs that keep them sitting upright and yet unable to move, like walker chairs without the wheels. Again, a staff member takes Baby from me, and puts her into an unoccupied seat. I wish she had not done this; why must Baby be forced to feel confined like that again? Immediately, Baby begins reaching out, toward the hand of the child sitting next to her, lifting as high as she can out of the constricting device until she is leaning over, and begins patting her neighbor's arm, and trying to touch the child's face. I watch in stunned silence. My God, I think, she is trying to comfort this child. It is clear these babies have learned to communicate with and draw strength from each other. They must; it is a matter of survival, for there is no other source.

I look around, but none of the others from the group are here to witness this. It is just me, the staff member, and the babies, and a sudden loneliness arises within me. I desperately want to get out of this place. Then Anna appears in the doorway and announces it is time to go, and I pull Baby hastily from the chair and hold her up in front of her friend. "Say good-bye, Baby; maybe you'll meet again someday," I tell her, and her little arm waves a bit as we walk toward the doorway, followed by the lonely eyes of that silent child.

The others in the group are already moving out to the plaza, but I hesitate inside. I notice Alex is sitting on the steps outside, her head in her hands. She seems distressed and yet I linger, there seems to be something I should do, some commemorative act to perform before carrying Baby from this place. This is a highly symbolic moment in an experience that is full of symbolism, and I hold Baby close, her head next to mine. I notice a set of double doors, with one door propped open to reveal a courtyard behind the building. I step to the threshold, which opens out into a trash-strewn, overgrown yard surrounded by the high walls of the orphanage building. In contrast to the front entrance with its pavement of beautiful stone, this weed-choked wasteland tells the true tale of this place.

Baby and I stand looking out over the forgotten field. I feel an enormous hot pressure rise in my chest, and all the emotion I have been holding back comes surging forth, my heart pounding, my head throbbing as the sadness of this place overwhelms my ability to keep the emotion at bay. Baby is calm and alert, as if she is waiting for something. I whisper a prayer of anguish, the anguish I feel for these children we will leave behind. Where is this pain to go? I cannot keep it inside me; I cannot take it outside these walls. Silent, fervent prayers must go somewhere. Who else to pray to, then, but Mary, the iconic mother of us all?

"Mary, oh, Mary," I plead. "What about these children?" The tears are pouring down my face now, hot and urgent. The enormity, the enormity of this . . . what human being could turn on their heels and walk away? And yet, I will do just that, I have to do just that. I have witnessed something that will haunt me as I sit at my kitchen table drinking coffee in suburbia, as I watch the privileged children at play in the neighborhood park; I will want to tell the mothers there about all these children lying uncared-for in metal cribs, longing for any type of human warmth or contact. But how will I do so without guilt? I am walking away too.

But then I remember—when I walk away, I will be holding tightly to one of these babies; one warm beating heart saved for the world. I close my eyes against the ugliness, against the human potential wasted inside these walls.

Instantly, a scene of powerful beauty fills my mind. The field before me is no longer a wasteland, but is transformed into an oasis of flowering trees, and lush grass. The sky is no longer colorless, but a deep clear blue. And then, thousands of glowing white doves swoop down from that sky, through the dilapidated courtyard, and into the dark cold rooms of the orphanage. The peaceful glow of the doves fills the rooms, their breath warms the air. Above each crib alights one dove to protect the sleeping child below. The Virgin Mary hovers above all, her outstretched arms filled with fragrant white lilies, glowing with unearthly light. "I would not forsake my children," she says. "I have been here all along."

I open my eyes as this image fades from my mind. I am overcome with gratitude for the vision that let me see past my own despair. How long have I been standing here? Am I hallucinating? If so, it seems a supremely sane response to such tragedy. I am oddly comforted by this vision, the burden on my chest is gone, my mind is peaceful and still. I know now that it is time, and I walk out into the hazy sunshine of the plaza to rejoin the group. I feel a lightness, a certainty, that my being in this place is not an accident.

What has just transpired seems to confer upon me a complete responsibility for this child. I walk carefully across the cobblestones, knowing that in my arms I hold a treasure beyond price, a jewel found twinkling in a pile of rubble.

∽

Curtis and Judy's baby cries all the way from the orphanage back to Nanchang. For two hours, nothing calms her. She is crying tears for all of us, a sadness we cannot express. Even Maggie is silent and subdued; there are no songs from Sunday school, or telling jokes with Curtis. She sits in the back of the van with her parents and new baby sister, watching the countryside roll by, with a blank expression on her face.

Earlier today her mother told us in a very matter-of-fact way that the orphanage where they got Maggie, in southern China, is far worse than the one we just saw. The babies sleep in wooden crates, and only straw covers the dirt floor. Just like a manger, I thought, and flicked my eyes to Maggie's face, which had gone suddenly masklike and immobile. A wall had gone up inside her, protecting her from this information. It was too much for a six-year-old to contemplate.

Alex and I don't speak during the ride back. When Baby and I rejoined her outside the orphanage on the plaza, she said, "I'm really feeling sick."

"What's wrong?" I asked, feeling nauseous myself, lightheaded and weak.

"I don't know," she answered. "I think it was that place. I wish we hadn't come."

I am so very glad we went, I think, so very glad. What if I had gone on about my life, not knowing of that, not understanding that, not seeing those babies? I shudder at the thought that I might have lived in eternal ignorance of this particular suffering. In some way that I can't explain, I feel that my entire life has been lived to bring me to this moment, the moment of seeing that place.

When we first got back in the van, I gave Alex a granola bar and some water, and that helped, she said. I am holding Baby, who is calmly chewing on a shortbread biscuit, her eyes big and bright. She is quiet, so quiet and self-possessed. I talk to her without speaking, she answers me without sound, we are sharing some private psychic space where I can feel her every feeling, and she mine. I watch as rice paddy fields flow by outside the window.

When we arrive back at the hotel and are on the way to our rooms, Jimmy says that he and Louise want to go out shopping later if anyone would like to go. Alex says no, but I tell Jimmy I want to go along, and we agree to meet in a couple of hours. We go to our rooms and I get Baby ready to take a nap. Alex lies down on her bed and I lie down on mine with Baby, and give her the bottle as she lies on my chest. Before long we are all deeply asleep, trying to put the disturbing images and gut-wrenching emotions of the orphanage visit behind us, and knowing we never will.

❧

I sat for some time among the roses and sweet-smelling jasmine. Han's face came to my mind again and again; I heard his voice, heard him speak the words that touched my heart. Something moved in me, and I felt again that which I had felt as Han and I sat together in the dappled sunlight of the pine grove. I felt that I must help him in some way, that I had been called to do so.

I closed my eyes and breathed in the night air. Its coolness made me alert to all sensations, to each thing inside and outside of me that could be reached by my awareness. I breathed and felt my mind clearing of all thought while I focused with attention upon a light inside, and the light grew larger and more luminous with each breath, until at last, I saw it, my master's face, just as he had said. I could reach him when I wished.

"Master," I said without speaking, with my thoughts, "I want to tell you of my meeting today."

"And do you think I do not know of it?" came the answer, from inside me, like a thought.

"I should not have doubted it! But what does it mean? Master, who is this man, the one they call Han?" I asked.

"You know in your heart who this man is. He is one who will work for the good, and that is all you need to know. You have come together because of your desire to help the people, and you shall have opportunity to do so in time. Please be patient, and follow your heart's guidance in this," replied the master.

"Master, I received a vision today, a vision of blessings being bestowed upon me. Can you tell me of this? What does it mean?"

"My child, each decision that you make carries with it the seeds of joy, or the seeds of despair. You have made a choice that will be of a magnitude undreamed of by you at this time. The blessings are yours by this choice, and will be kept for you forever in the vaults of heaven, and will rain to you on earth as such time allows."

I felt a chill ripple throughout my body at these words, words I did not fully understand, but did not doubt. Pulling my robe around me more tightly, I left the garden to spend the night dreaming fitfully upon my little bed, dreaming of legions of angels, and a small black-haired baby, who reached out her arms to me.

∽

A black-haired baby . . . what was that dream? I struggle to throw off the last shreds of dream consciousness as I rise with Baby from the narrow bed. Alex is still sleeping, and as I move about the room, I wonder about the man in the dream, about the feeling of deep connection with him.

Fatigue is starting to take its toll on all of us now. The grueling trip, the sleepless first two nights with the new babies, and the visit to the orphanage have left us all drained. But compared to the others, I am feeling energetic, probably because of the fifteen-hour sleep marathon two nights before. I feel a need to move, and start bustling around the room with Baby. Alex wakes up and says in a groggy voice from her bed, "I can't get up." I offer to let Alex rest while I take Baby out into the city with Jimmy, Louise, Maggie, and Livvy, their new baby.

Before we leave the hotel room, I put Baby into her stroller and prepare the diaper bag with her necessities: bottle of formula, snack, blanket, diapers, wipes, toys. I have never cared for an infant before, and yet oddly, I know just what to do for Baby.

I am in high spirits as we get ready to go, though I can't explain why. When we leave the room, Alex is lying in her bed, head totally under the covers, drapes drawn against the light, and we go quietly so as not to disturb her sleep.

Jimmy flags down a taxi in front of our hotel, and the six of us pile in. Jimmy and Louise want to go to a department store they know of, one they visited the last time they were here, when they adopted Maggie. The city is teeming with life: people riding bicycles or pushing carts with children in them, cars and trucks zigzagging through the streets, horns blaring. People are everywhere, so many people. I had thought Nanchang was a small provincial backwater, but I asked Anna and she said the population is three million. There are high-rise buildings, modern vehicles, and a beautiful promenade along the river. And yet, as the cab enters a traffic rotary, I look over to see a dirty peasant man holding a stick twice as tall as he is, driving a huge pink sow and her six piglets around the circle, merging with the vehicle traffic. It is so funny and unexpected, and Maggie and I start to giggle together uncontrollably when I point it out to her.

Most of the buildings are dingy and run-down, with lines of laundry hanging from almost every window. Underwear and socks hang next to dead ducks and sausages left out to cure. When my mind adjusts to these strange juxtapositions, I feel a strange exhilaration, a raw energy picked up from these streets, where life is being lived at its most unrefined. I like the ragged edges that are showing here, and I look around with avid enjoyment at the spectacle outside my window.

We drive across town. It takes about a half hour before we pull up in front of a large square building set behind a wide paved plaza, a row of red banners flapping happily above the entrance. Lots of people are milling about the plaza, and as soon as we open the doors and step out of the cab, we are thronged by a crowd trying to catch a glimpse of the foreigners who have just arrived on the scene. There is no understanding of respect for privacy, or personal boundaries. People crowd right up to us, looking straight into our faces with no smiles, with no acknowledgment of our right to space so that we can maneuver our way into the building. It is like they are inspecting exotic zoo animals, and they try to get as close as they can.

It is a surprise to suddenly be in such close proximity to so many people. Until now, we have been protected from onlookers by Anna, by the walls and windows of the van, by the controlled confines of the hotel. Now we are in the midst of a crowd, with nothing to buffer us from each other, on our first outing without Anna. They look at our clothes, listen intently to us speak, watch how we handle the babies. Some women come up and pull on the pants leg of Louise's baby, and pantomime their displeasure that she is not dressed warmly enough. The Chinese bundle their babies in layers and layers of warm clothing, with no skin showing, and Louise's baby has only a thin jacket, and skin is showing between the trouser leg and the top of her sock, a parenting sin.

Jimmy and Louise move away quickly toward the entrance, and I start to panic—I am still struggling to open the stroller that Alex brought for the baby, I can't follow. The proximity of these strangers, none of whom look like me or can understand me if I speak, frightens me. I am afraid I will lose Jimmy and Louise in the crowd and not be able to find my way back to the hotel. What would I do, lost alone in this city with the baby? I can't even pronounce the name of our hotel. Never in all my travels have I felt this kind of visceral fear, a feeling that there is nothing to fall back on.

Finally Jimmy notices I am not behind them, and pushes back through the crowd and takes my arm, leading me and Baby through the sea of people and into the department store. We wheel the babies around the displays of merchandise. People openly stare, and I wonder what they are thinking. Are they resentful of these Americans adopting Chinese children? Are they supportive? Curious? Earlier I asked Anna about this, and she said that most Chinese would see these adoptions as a very good thing.

"They would think these are, uh . . ." she said, casting about for just the right word, ". . . ee-ro." She shook her head, correcting herself, "Hero!"

When she said it, I wondered if that could be true, that the Chinese see the adopting parents as heroes. There are bound to be mixed, ambivalent feelings about this phenomenon. What I notice more than anything on people's faces is a sort of bewilderment: what is going on here, why are American people carting around Chinese babies? Perhaps they really don't know what is going on; the press is censored here. There are surely no stories in the papers about large numbers of abandoned children or about the foreigners who come to adopt a small number of them.

I read that the Chinese president Jiang Zemin had himself been adopted as a child and that he was responsible for opening China to international adoption in the early nineties because his own adoption experience was so positive. But then why only promote international adoptions, and not domestic ones, within China? There is no domestic adoption program in China to speak of, but a thriving business in international adoptions has taken hold.

I stop with Baby in front of a jewelry display case and look at the jade jewelry arrayed inside. Maybe I should buy Baby some jade for her to keep. What would be nice? I indicate to the salesgirl behind the counter that I would like to see a tiny bracelet, a circle of smooth jade with a golden clasp. I have seen other babies wearing these bracelets; Anna told me they are for protection from evil spirits. I look up and the salesgirl looks at me, then down at the baby in the stroller, then back at me again. Struggling for the right words, she stammers, "You—you baby?"

For the sake of ease, I answer, "Yes; my baby."

"Lucky baby, go to America," she says. "Lucky baby." She says this wistfully, without smiling. Yes, yes. Lucky baby.

Lucky Baby and I wheel through the bedding displays next, then the shoe department, and then cosmetics. The beauty counters are presided over by a larger-than-life-size poster of

Cindy Crawford, hawking Revlon. She is ubiquitous; it is impossible to avoid her image even here in Nanchang, China. What good, I wonder, could the image of Cindy Crawford possibly do for these women? Couldn't Revlon use Asian faces to sell its beauty products to Asian women? It would just be the courteous thing to do, especially here, where a tube of lipstick might cost the equivalent of a week's wages at the shoestring factory.

I am in a daze, a fog of surrealism. Is this happening, am I in China, wheeling a baby around a department store? Did Alex really ask me last night if I would take this baby? Take this baby, raise this baby . . . Lucky Baby, how lucky would that be for you? Am I the person who can be your mother, can I be the person that you need me to be?

I lean down to look Baby in the eye. Her big, round eyes, accentuated by the knit cap, are deep, dark, somber. Her face is all eyes, all windows of a soul I cannot fathom.

"So," I whisper, "is it going to be me and you, then?" I am trying this idea out in my mind, to see how it feels. I am asking her, I am asking myself, what would it take, could we do this? We look deeply at each other, the question already answered.

ovm

After leaving the department store, Jimmy, Louise, Maggie, and I, and the babies, take a taxi to a riverfront hotel that is rumored to have the best American-style hamburgers in the city. The lobby is decorated for Christmas, with a tall fake evergreen trimmed in red velvet bows. American Christmas music plays over the speakers in the almost-empty dining room, reminding me for a moment how far we are from home.

The waiter takes our order: "ba-sgetti" for Maggie, and burgers for the rest of us. We talk then; Jimmy tells me about their life at home, and what it's been like to raise a little Chinese girl in a small town.

"People can be rude," he says. "I get asked all the time, 'Where did you get her?' Right in front of her, like she can't even hear them. She sticks out like a sore thumb there."

"Really?" I ask. I had not thought of this. Where I live, a Chinese girl, even with Caucasian parents, would not look out of place.

"It's why we came back for a second child," he continues. "So she won't feel so alone. She's the only Asian in her school—hell, maybe in the whole town."

I look at Maggie, sitting across the table, banging her spoon against the china plate and singing with her lisp, "Joy to the world! The Lord hath come . . ." along with the piped-in music track. The distinctiveness doesn't seem to have held her back. In fact, she seems to revel in attention of any kind.

Then he asks me why I came on this trip. "So, what are you doing here?" is how he puts it. I laugh a little, and tell him, "I wish I knew!"

"Seriously, though," I go on, "I thought it would be interesting to see how this whole international adoption process works."

"Why didn't her husband come? It's kind of strange. . . ." he begins.

Luckily the food arrives, interrupting us; I don't want to talk about Alex. We dig into our "American" hamburgers that taste exactly like soy sauce. I feed little bits of the burger to Baby, and she gobbles them up, one after the other; she is ravenous. When we run out of burger, she eats rice, noodles, vegetables, anything I offer. My appetite is nowhere near as robust as hers. I am glad to see her eating, gaining strength with each passing hour, the thin thread connecting her to life becoming more and more substantial.

And then I understand. Until now, I have not been able to identify exactly what I saw in Baby's eyes that first night. Something like grief, I thought, or sadness, though neither seemed quite right. Now I know, she was just barely hanging on to life.

Baby would not make it if she went back to the orphanage. Her will to live would not survive a return to those conditions. Surely, infants too can reach a point of not wanting to struggle anymore. To be in a world with no love or warmth, hungry and cold all the time, where no one cares particularly about you . . . Surely at some point they give up, not willing to fight for such a harsh existence any longer. How many of these abandoned babies just wither away after a time?

Being removed from the only place she ever knew was clearly a shock. But after two days of someone holding her, feeding her, singing to her, and keeping her warm, she has already begun to blossom, to fight her way back to life. To send her back now to a life of deprivation would be a cruelty beyond belief.

All my stated reasons for coming on this trip are swept away with this understanding, and I know my true purpose is to prevent that cruelty, to stop that cycle of pain in at least one life, and with this chance I have been given, to redeem my own.

∼

In the backseat of a taxi on the way back to the hotel, Baby lies across my lap, looking up into my face, calm and satisfied. Maggie sits next to me, repeating the name of our hotel in the way the driver taught her when we got into the cab and said, "Jin Feng Hotel, please."

"Jee FONG! Jee FONG!" Maggie says in a tonal singsong voice, over and over, and for once her parents don't tell her to quiet down. We hurtle through the darkness, and I marvel at the strangeness of this trip, how none of it could have been predicted. It occurs to me that we never really know where our journeys may ultimately take us. We think we know, and try to prepare. We make plans and itineraries, pack clothing for certain types of weather. We take our bodies to specific geographical locations, but how often do we think of the effect it may have upon our souls? How often do we wonder, Why this destination, and not some other? Why have I chosen it, or has it chosen me? What part of myself awaits me there, where I am going?

Traveling to China from the United States is a long journey, but I had no way of knowing how far inside myself I would travel by coming here. A day's journey that took me to a forgotten lifetime; in the end, I don't know exactly where I am or how to return to the life I have left. The confusion of being on the other side of the world has forced me to see things differently. China sleeps while we are awake, our biological clocks set at exactly opposite poles. Their night of remembering is our day of forgetting; we speak a different language of time. The American and Chinese collective minds swirl in opposite directions, ours toward the future, and theirs toward the past.

During this journey I have lost a day, and will gain it back upon my return. How does this happen, time getting lost? Think too deeply about the absurdities of this and it becomes apparent that the human invention of time, of days following days in a tidy linear progression, is an illusion, a trick we forget we have played upon ourselves. We are conditioned to accept time as an absolute, and yet, in one sense there is no time at all.

It is always now, and everywhere that exists, exists now. Though in one place the sun is shining and it is called "Tuesday morning," at the very same moment in some other geographical location it is dark and we say, "Wednesday." A day ahead? No; the same moment, exactly. Tuesday and Wednesday, happening at the same time. Past and future, dark and light, today and tomorrow, always inseparable.

⌇

It is late when Baby and I return to the hotel room. Alex opens the door, a pinched look of exhaustion on her face.

"I haven't slept at all," she says, "or eaten anything. I feel worse than ever." She says that after we left, she lay in bed and couldn't stop her mind from whirling, from turning the situation over and over in her head.

"I'm feeling panicked again," she says. Standing in the darkened room, just inside the door, with her hair disheveled and in her nightclothes, she reminds me of a ghost.

"What does that mean?" I ask her, still holding Baby, rocking her gently back and forth to keep her calm, though I'm feeling anything but.

"I just can't get past the feeling that this isn't right," she says. "I can't do it. I can't take the baby."

I walk into the room and sit down with Baby on the bed. I expected that when we returned, Alex would greet us feeling rested, feeling better, ready to put this all behind her. Now it is obvious that her doubts were not transitory misgivings. Two days have gone by, with no real attempt to bond with the baby.

I sit in silence for a long moment. Alex still cannot express exactly why she feels she can't take Baby, but I know the reason. She doesn't love her; it is as simple as that. As unbelievable as it is to me, she does not love this child, and feels that she never will. She should not have her, I think. It is correct that she not take her to a life with no real love.

"Will you take her?" she asks. Her tone is desperate.

Will I take her? Last night, when I told Alex that I would take the baby, I was trying to be helpful, to give her some breathing room until her doubts and fears subsided. It was easy to say then. I didn't really believe it would happen. But now I know she has decided whether to keep this child; she will not. She is really asking me if I will do this, if I will take this child as my own.

I look around the darkened room and note the little built-in beds, the crib in the corner, our clothes and belongings scattered about. A cramped, dreary little room in Nanchang, China . . . One never knows where one's life might change forever.

The question, Will you take her? hangs in the air between us, and everything I have ever aspired to be, all the lessons I have ever learned, all the pain I have ever felt, crystallize around it, transforming it into the real question: Will you love her?

"Yes," I say. "I will."

~

I take Baby out into the hallway, around and around on our well-worn path, while Alex calls her husband to tell him that no baby will be coming home. Did I actually just agree to take a baby? Just like that? I've taken longer to decide about buying a pair of shoes than I did to decide this, the most important decision I have ever made. Why was this so easy, why no fear or hesitation? I search inside myself for some shred of doubt, and find nothing, nothing but an open feeling, a spaciousness in my heart, clear and deep, a cloudless blue sky. In the moment I said

I would take her, I felt the sanest I have ever been in my life. An exquisite balance between head and heart, neither driven by emotion nor halted by thought, it was the purest yes I have said to anything, ever. A drink of pure water for my own parched and thirsty soul, I drank it down, yes, yes, to life. Yes to love, with no guarantees.

⌇

After Alex talks to her husband, she asks me to call mine.

"I want to know this is set tonight. I won't be able to sleep if you haven't talked to him. He's going to have to agree for you to be able to adopt her," she says. I say I will, but I ask, "Just give me a few minutes; I need to think through what I'm going to tell him."

"Fine," she says, and I hand Baby to her and go out into the hallway.

I sit down in the spot where I held Baby last night, after Alex told me she didn't want her. With my back against the wall, I breathe deeply, trying to calm myself, thinking about my husband, my marriage, the many years we've had together. We just celebrated our fourteenth wedding anniversary three months ago; that evening we talked about how great it was going to be now that his daughter was away at college and we had the house to ourselves. She had lived with us for three tumultuous years, her high school years, and we were both worn out from it. He wanted, he said, "peace and quiet for a while."

But surely he will see that a baby's life takes precedence over any plans we have made? I think about what might happen to her if Alex did send her back to the orphanage. Would she suffer even more neglect, more cruelty, because she had been rejected, because she was deemed unacceptable by an American?

My fear is that that is exactly what would happen to her, and I shiver as I think of the bleak existence she would face. I know from my talks with Anna that the children chosen for adoption are selected very carefully, and that a rejection is an embarrassment for which the agency would most likely blame the child. A child already abandoned . . . and then rejected again; I wonder if there is a Chinese symbol for that, the opposite of the one for "double happiness"?

Somehow, I must make him see.

My hand shakes as I wait for my husband to pick up the phone. I have no idea what he will say, how he will react to this. I am scared because I know that no matter what he says, I have to bring this baby home.

He picks up the phone, his voice traveling a ridiculously long distance across tiny wires. He says hello, and I have never been so happy to hear his voice. In the four days since he left me at the airport, I have lived a lifetime.

"What are you doing calling? I thought you said we wouldn't talk until your birthday, when you are in Hong Kong!" he says, sounding perplexed.

"Well . . ." my hands are shaking, my voice is shaking, my stomach is fluttering, how do I say this? "This trip is not going as planned. . . ."

"What happened, is everything all right? What's wrong?" He is serious now, he can tell by the tone of my voice that I am barely hanging on, that I am about to cry.

"Alex doesn't want this baby."

I hear myself say it, out loud, and it sounds awful, like I've just spoken an obscenity. There is silence. "Doesn't want this baby" echoes across the miles between us. I know that he hears this instantaneously, but it is as if there is a lag before the full impact hits him.

Silence. Silence. Silence. The moment draws out, an eternal moment, living another lifetime in just this instant. This is where questions might spontaneously arise, like "Why not?" or "What happened?" but there is nothing, no questions. Silence. And then:

"We'll take her," he says.

A feeling I have never experienced before, a spontaneous and mindless joy, floods over me. I am sobbing and laughing and babbling into the phone, "Oh my god, she's beautiful, the sweetest thing ever, she's perfect for us, I know you will love her. . . ."

"I already do," he says.

"But how? Why? How can you just say yes like that, you haven't even seen her, you know nothing about her. . . ."

"I know *you*. If you say this is the right thing, then it's the right thing. I trust you," he says, and it changes everything. This is trust bought with years of my life, years I sometimes thought were wasted. What is trust worth? In this case, a baby's life.

"Whatever else you do in life, it will never be better than this," I tell him, and it is done.

He has always been a person who loves children, the first one to grab a bat and ball and start a game at a family gathering when all the other adults are ignoring the kids; the first one to approach a shy child at one of his kids' school functions. I have accused him over the years of liking children more than adults, and he has never even attempted to argue the point.

But more than just "liking" children, there is a vulnerability from his own childhood, a tender wound that he seeks to heal by reaching out to kids he thinks might be in danger of being

wounded, of being rejected. He cannot stand to see a child rejected, and I should have known that he would not be able to
turn away from this one, one he can help.

There are logistics to be discussed, we don't even know if it's
legally possible to do this; and yet, our relationship is complete
in this moment, and there is a feeling that together we can
make this, or anything, happen.

After we hang up, I go to the door and motion for Alex to
come back into the room. She has Baby, and as she enters she
hands her to me.

"What did he say?" she asks anxiously, searching my face
with her eyes.

"He said, 'bring her home'; he wants to do it," I answer as I
hug Baby to me.

"Oh, I am so relieved!" Alex exclaims. "I was so worried he
would say no."

I don't tell her that I was worried too. I just say, "He said he
was going to call your husband right away, and they were going
to figure out a way to make this happen."

She looks genuinely pleased, happy for the first time since
this trip began. We all get ready for bed. Baby is bubbly too, the
mood is infectious. When we get into bed, a wave of exhaustion
carries me off to sleep, the words "bring her home, bring her
home," echoing in my mind.

ↄ

*A bell sounded. At once, a line of people surged forth toward some-
thing I could not see. They pushed each other, men shoving women,
women knocking into children, pushing forward into the shelter. Cries
of desperation were heard, the wail of a child took on the high pitch of
fear. Other people began streaming in from all sides, people who had*

not been standing in the line, but now sought to take advantage of the disorder provoked by the sounding of the bell. I half stood in the carriage, putting my head through the window opening to better see the melee taking place. Fighting had broken out. . . . Some men had formed a knot of flailing limbs. Grunts and shouts rose from their midst, and then someone was thrown from the throng and onto his head into the dirt. A small stream of blood oozed from a gash in his head, and he did not move. No one came to his aid as the crowd surged farther into the shelter.

Uniformed men had now arrived and surrounded the building. Some moved forward and began hitting those in the crowd that they could reach with their long sticks. As they were hit, the victims fell, holding their heads or arms, crying or cursing or sitting silently in dejection. A woman, holding a baby, tried to move forward around the outer edge of the crowd. A man turned and pushed her, causing her to bump forcefully into one of the uniformed men. I saw him raise his stick, raise his arm high, and bring it down with force upon the shoulders of the woman, and she fell, her baby tumbling a few feet away from her in the dirt.

"Stop! Stop this at once!" The cry came from somewhere deep inside. The power and volume of my shout caused all eyes to turn toward the carriage, where I had flung open the door and jumped into the street. A stunned Shiu Lin still sat inside, clutching at the curtain. The eunuchs stood with mouths wide, unsure of what they were witnessing. And the military guards began looking toward their officers for direction, and none came. The officers were looking at me in surprise, Han among them. I saw him from the corner of my eye as I moved toward the baby that still lay on the gritty street.

༄

"Stop! Stop this at once!" I wake some hours later and look at the clock: two a.m. Cries of desperation echo in my head, the remnants of an intense dream still reverberating in my consciousness. It was somewhere unfamiliar . . . a marketplace, a street filled with people . . . I was riding in a carriage, and then something happened: a baby?

I think about calling my friend Josephine, to tell her about the dreams and all that has happened, but I didn't even bring her number; I never thought I would need to call her from China. But now I want to get her insight on these strange events, events that will change my life, one way or another. Baby is asleep, and, finally, so is Alex, so I get dressed and leave the room, headed for the lobby, where I can have some privacy.

Josephine and I spoke for the first time just three months ago. My friend Claire insisted that I call her, pressing her phone number into my hand as we sat in her garden on a sunlit morning in early fall. Claire and I had met in a yoga class a year before, and from the first evening, I knew we would be friends; within weeks we were as comfortable with each other as sisters, part of each other's lives.

Many of my other friendships of much longer duration have never evolved to this state; like my friendship with Alex, for instance. I have known Alex for over ten years, but there is something in me that has remained wary of her, though I am not able to say why.

On the morning when she spoke to me of Josephine, Claire and I had been talking about the practice of psychology. I had been telling her that there seems to be something missing in all the techniques and theories, and I don't know how much psychology is really helping people. I have been working as a counselor for a couple of years and have become disillusioned with the promise of psychotherapy. Understand the mind and problems will be solved, goes the theory; but somehow in practice it never seems to work out that way.

Perhaps psychotherapy is a dead end, I said to Claire, and there needs to be something more for people to truly heal. After sitting for hundreds of hours with clients suffering from every imaginable permutation of misery, I have begun to sense that the dysfunctional behaviors, the longings, the pain, have some sort of underlying logic or meaning that is impossible to discover with the conventional tools of therapy.

"I think you should talk to Josephine," she said, though when I pressed her she could not tell me why. Claire had known Josephine for years, and had mentioned her many times to me. But she had never really offered details about her, and she didn't seem to want to that morning, either. It all seemed somewhat mysterious, and I was skeptical.

Claire said that Josephine had an interesting way of looking at these issues, and had made them her life's work. She seemed to feel strongly that Josephine and I should talk, so I did call, the next afternoon. When Josephine answered, her charming English accent was the first surprise, the first of many. One of the first things she said to me was, "Things are not as they appear."

Things are not as they appear. All of my searching over the years had led to dead ends. My study of psychology, science, religious thought, yoga, and Buddhism had led me to a place where I had to accept that there was something more, something beyond my understanding, something not explained fully in any of the books I read. What the "something more" was, I had no idea. I still had no explanation for it, and it haunted me.

"What do you want, what are you looking for?" Josephine

asked, questions no one had ever asked before, at least not so directly. She asked the only questions that matter. She told me that she worked as a spiritual guide and teacher. I told her that she was exactly what I was looking for, though until the moment those words came out of my mouth, I had not known it was true.

"Josephine, I'm looking for the real thing," I said, hesitating, not knowing if she would understand what I meant, not knowing for sure if I knew what I meant.

Josephine laughed. And when she laughed, it sounded like the tinkling of bells I had heard in a dream—long, long ago.

From that point on we have spoken at least once a week on the telephone, our conversations always intense and sometimes going on for hours. Josephine studied many years at what she called an "Ancient Mystery School," where she learned about metaphysics, prayer, and meditation. Oftentimes I told her about my dreams, which were intense and seemed filled with a symbolism I could not decipher, and together we explored the possible meanings and information the dreams were imparting.

When I first told her of my plan to accompany Alex to China, she told me in no uncertain terms that I should not go. The reasons, she said, had to do with certain energies that have amassed in certain locations, due to the attitudes and mass karma of the people. "Like walking into a hornet's nest!" was how she put it; and she told me that the negativity and oppression in China might affect me deeply in ways I could not predict.

"I have to go," I said. "I made a commitment to Alex, I can't pull out of this now." She conceded it would be difficult, and suggested that I take her phone number with me. Why had I not done it? I am standing in a phone booth, wondering how to get her number, when I see it, in my mind's eye: her number right there, and I pick up the phone and dial, and within moments she is on the other end of the line.

I tell her, "Oh, Josephine, you are not going to believe this. . . ." and I begin explaining how this trip has become an incredible journey.

"She asked me to take the baby," I finally say.

There is silence on the other end of the line. I wait, and become aware that this is not the silence of surprise, but that she is praying, that she is checking in with what she refers to as "the Heavens," her guides in the spirit realm from whom she gets information.

"And what did you say?" she finally asks, quietly, expectantly.

"I said I would. I agreed to take her," I answer, and I hear her let out her breath on the other end, a great sigh. "Oh, God," she says. "Remember when I asked you a few weeks ago if you wanted me to come on this trip with you? I knew something of significance was going to happen, I just didn't know what."

It was true. She did offer to come, and it seemed so strange to me at the time. Josephine did not know Alex at all, and this trip really wasn't about me. She didn't explain why she felt she should come, and the issue was dropped and we haven't spoken of it again, until now. And now I wonder, what did she know, what did she see?

"Josephine, that's not all; I've been having dreams, strange dreams while I've been here, almost every night. I can't put my finger on it, but these dreams are all about China—maybe it's connected somehow."

"Have you written them down?" she asks. I tell her I have written some, but since Alex told me she didn't want the baby, I haven't been able to. "Write them down, and call me back if you can," she says, and I agree to call her back; just talking to her has made me feel much better. But one thing she says sticks in my mind and causes concern: she tells me to pray for protection, for myself and for Baby, until we are safely home, until we are out of China.

⌇

As I lie in bed in the darkened room, my mind leaps from thought to thought, from mundane concerns about diapers and bottles and cribs, to sublime visions of our new family unit. My friends and family will think I'm totally nuts—I go to China and bring back a baby! No one will be expecting this, I wasn't even expecting this. Am I crazy? Wouldn't a normal person have some doubts, some hesitation? But I have none.

I want to meditate, to see if any insight will come. I breathe deeply and sink deeper into my self, into the calm center I have learned how to find, into my heart. I can feel it beating its steady rhythm, never failing me, always there to be found. Breathing, breathing, I let go of the rim of consciousness, I fall in . . . into that secret place, where everything is known.

Something emerges, out of the darkness. I see her shining as she comes forward; and she is holding something in her arms. It is the Virgin Mary, and she is holding a child in her arms. Beside her stands my own late mother, smiling with uncontained delight. They are looking at me, and Mary moves forward; she hands the child to me. She hands the child to me, and I look down and it is Baby, the child is Baby, and Mary has handed her to me. I look up, into the Mother's eyes, and she lifts her arms once again and places a wreath of white lilies upon my head. And she speaks.

"I am giving her to you," she says. "I am giving this blessed child to you."

The image fades and I am stunned with happiness; I am in awe at what I have seen. My mother has been dead these past six years. For six years I have thought I was without her. But now I see she has been with me, she has come to my inner sight, to comfort me, to show me that all is well, and to confirm that no more questions need to be asked.

৩৯

"Where am I?" I asked, struggling to sit upright, looking around me. Behind me stood a grove of pine, ancient and noble. Before me was a pool of dark water, ringed with blooming water lilies, reflecting their blossoms in its depths. Butterflies played at the edges of the water, and bees hurried from blossom to blossom. On the far side of the pool stood a lovely pagoda, its graceful lines echoing its own reflection. I felt peace, a peace I had not known since my days in the forest near my village, when Chen and I would pick berries and mushrooms, happily losing ourselves in the beauty of nature.

"You have come to Black Dragon Pool, Mistress. It is to be yours. . . . This reflecting pool has been reserved for the Empress since ancient times, and as you will become Empress tomorrow upon your marriage, you may enjoy its peace and tranquility now, when it appears you so badly need it," said Han.

"I shall become Empress tomorrow," I repeated, and at those words the fear and nausea gripped me.

I stood up abruptly. "I cannot do it," I said, looking Han full in the face.

Han jumped up, alarmed. "You cannot do it? But, what do you mean?"

"I cannot become Empress," I said, and moved to go past him. As I

*did so, I wavered and lost my balance, and crumpled down once again
to the soft grass, still weak and exhausted. Han steadied me, holding my
arm and guiding me back so that I lay upon the ground, the crimson
gown pooled out around me.*

*"You must become Empress, it is too late to change that. The Em-
peror would not take kindly to being jilted by his chosen bride, of that I
can assure you. And what could you be thinking, to want to turn aside
this honor?" Han asked. He reached forward and pushed aside from my
forehead a lock of hair that had escaped my coiffure. His fingers brushed
my skin and I felt an energy linger there; a warmth, a tenderness.*

*"In a vision, I saw a black cloud descend upon me. If I become Em-
press, I will not survive it, I will not survive," I answered, shivering
from the remembrance of the darkness in that cloud.*

*Han was silent for a moment, carefully considering my words. "But
of course, as Empress you will have everything necessary to your well-
being at your disposal," Han said, trying to reassure me. "You are overwhelmed with the enormity of the wedding preparations now, but that
will subside. And besides, I shall help you, should you need anything,
anything at all."*

*His face showed an unmistakable sincerity, a softness toward me
that took me by surprise. "You shall help me? But why? Why should
you trouble yourself with my needs?" I asked urgently, grabbing his
hand where it lay in the grass before me. "And why should you choose
to accompany me today?" His hand was dry and warm, and I felt him
jerk slightly at my touch, not expecting it to come. Han looked at me
with luminous eyes as I held his hand there, on my lap, not letting go.*

"Mistress," he began. "What happened yesterday, in the market—"

*"Yes, yes I know; you are angry with me for my words, for my bold
usurpation of authority!" I interrupted him, eager to explain. "But you
must know, I did not think. . . . I merely acted with an instinct of care for
the woman I saw there, with the child."*

"But that is just it!" Han cried. "You acted, not from tradition or with a thought for acceptable behavior. You acted from the heart, and with courage. And in that moment, I thought of you as I have never thought of a woman before: I saw you as a warrior, a kindred spirit to my own. And I thought what a fine Empress you would make, and vowed to be in your service."

I was struck silent at his words. A man such as Han, pledged to my service? But what could this mean? How could he protect me, in what way could he help? I was to be married tomorrow, and had seen the black cloud descend; and yet Han was reassuring me that all would be well.

I lifted my head to reply and saw his face before me, so close I could feel his breath upon my cheek. "We must go back now," he said. "You are expected in the Emperor's chambers."

Han brought his lips to mine and gently pressed them there, and I did not move. My heart pounded in my chest, and all else was silence.

∽

Neither Alex nor Baby is awake in the morning when I rise from bed, dress, and go to the hotel restaurant in search of breakfast, and coffee. On the way down in the elevator, snatches of a dream from last night rise to the surface, one after the other: standing at the edge of some sort of lake or pool; an intense exchange with a young Chinese man. It seemed he was someone who would protect me, but from what, I can't quite recall. Something had happened, I had become frightened during some ceremony or ritual, and he had brought me to a place to calm me. He called me "Mistress," but I do not remember what I called him. I do remember his saying I would become Empress, and the feeling that brought was one of sheer terror. Stepping from the elevator, the dream memory fades as I notice the sign pointing to the restaurant and go inside, where there is an enormous buffet arranged in the middle of the room.

For the first time in two days I am hungry, and I fill my plate with eggs, bacon, bread, and fruit from the buffet and sit alone at a small table. Everything tastes so good, like I am eating for the first time, but it is really just that I'm eating for the first time while being happy.

And I am—happy. The thought of bringing Baby home fills me with curious delight, with exhilaration, and all night I was in and out of sleep, thinking about Baby, how my life will change, how I did not know before how much I wanted it to change. It wasn't until I said that I would take Baby that I realized how much I wanted her. I took a leap of faith, and my heart opened up like a parachute, and I made a safe landing, firm on solid ground.

A pure thing, happening by chance or by grace, took me by surprise and ran around my defenses. I would have to give her everything, my whole self, and what would that be like? Always before, in matters of love, I held back, was cautious; not giving to the full extent seemed wise and prudent, the smart thing to do. Now it seems stunted and sad. The longing I have always had was for this, this one pure thing. Whatever happens now, whether she comes to me or not, I will always have that moment, the one moment when I said yes and meant it with my entire being.

I still cannot believe it, but oh . . . if the planets and stars whirl into alignment, if all obstacles crumble, if there is a God, a benevolent God, and Baby is to be mine, the life we can live together will be a different kind of life than I have ever known.

I finish my breakfast and walk slowly across the lobby, engrossed in thought. It crosses my mind that many obstacles still remain and that the odds are against all the pieces of this puzzle falling into place. And yet I feel so strongly, so surely that it is done, that I will have Baby, and that no matter what arises she must be with me.

I glance at my watch. I have been gone a long time, almost two hours now, I had not realized. Going up in the elevator, I wonder how Baby slept. Is she awake yet? I cannot wait to see her again, to spend another day getting to know her, the baby that is going to be my child.

Letting myself into the room, I know immediately that something has changed. I open the door and feel the bustling energy in the room, see that the drapes have been pulled back to let in the morning light, the beds have been made, and Alex is moving around purposefully, tidying up her belongings. Both she and Baby are dressed, and Baby is sitting on a blanket on the floor, playing with a rattle. Something in the way Alex is moving, something in the energy, something even in the cute outfit she has put on Baby, tells me last night was just a dream, a foolish fantasy.

I stand just inside the doorway, reluctant to enter, a dread rising up, and with it the force of self-recriminating thoughts, the you-idiot-how-could-you-have-let-yourself-want-this-how-could-you-have-thought-this-could-really-happen-my-God-you-actually-let-yourself-believe-you-would-get-this-child-you-let-yourself-love-her unleashes in my mind.

Alex turns and sees me there. "Oh, I'm glad you're back!" she says, cheerfully, terrible in her cheerfulness. I wish she were a little bit sheepish, it would at least allow me to manufacture some compassion for her. But no, not to be. Even that is taken from me, by the terrible cheerfulness.

"I've been up for a while now, and I can't believe it, I feel so much better today! You know . . . I don't know why I was feeling like I couldn't take this baby. Today, I feel like I can do it!"

As if nothing has happened. As if she has not asked me to take this baby, to change my life, to commit in an instant. As if I have not said yes.

As if Baby were not my child.

"But I want to try it for today and see what happens. It doesn't mean that I'll definitely keep her."

She wants to try it for today, and see what happens. She wants to *try* it . . . what, what in God's name could she be thinking? So if it doesn't feel right today, I suppose she'll let me know tonight, and then the next morning, maybe she'll feel better again . . . and on and on. Every alarm bell in my psyche is clanging: be careful, be careful. Don't even give off a whiff of resistance to this, and don't try to reason with insanity.

I take a deep gulp of air, calm down, calm down. Some instinct takes over and I hear myself saying, "Well, I'm glad you're feeling better. That's great." Deep breath. I smile and wave at Baby, playing happily on the ground. A hard lump rises in my throat.

"I know, it is amazing. It's like I'm a different person! I guess all I needed was a good night's sleep," she exclaims.

She continues to prattle on, something—something about what to do today or eating breakfast or something. I'm not listening, deep in counsel with myself. What to do? There is only one option. I am so deflated and depleted right now that I have to get out. I have lost her, the child I hadn't even known I wanted.

"Alex, I just have to say . . . I'm feeling pretty drained after all this. Last night was emotional for me, I mean . . . my husband and I made plans to change our lives! And now all of it is in doubt, so I just need to step back, step away. You and the baby need some time to bond, and I can't just keep taking care of her for you. I can't stay engaged, wondering if you are going to want the baby or not want the baby. You need to decide. I'm going to spend the day by myself and let you be with her."

Alex says that she understands. It is odd, chilling, how easily she accepts her own change of mind. I would say change of heart, but I am certain that her heart still remains closed.

I start moving around the room, putting on my running clothes, getting my backpack together: books, notebook, pen. I can't wait to get out. Baby keeps trying to get my attention; I can't even look at her, it breaks my heart. I am abandoning her, leaving her with this woman who is not even sure that she wants her.

On the way out of the hotel I stash my backpack in the office off the lobby. Emerging into the hazy sunlight, into the dust and noise of the city, I am relieved. I feel relieved of an oppressive burden, the desires and dreams I was nurturing before I walked back into the room this morning. Those dreams have evaporated, have burned away with Alex's words.

All that remains is a distilled essence of love, love for that baby. I start running along the promenade, beside the river, the mighty Yangtze; people are staring, turning their heads as I pass by. I don't care, I just want to run and run and run, to go deeply into that essence of love.

Oh, God, please, please, let her go to the right place, please let her be happy. I am sobbing, tears welling into my eyes so that it is hard to see. What can I do? I am powerless; I have never felt so completely at the mercy of events. There is something I can do, someone I can love, and will I be allowed to? My heart is burning, I can feel the heat rise up in my chest, and a band grips and tightens there, making it hard to breathe.

The sky is dull gray and looks as if it could weep, but these are not the clouds of rain above my head, they are the clouds of dirt, of neglect, of greed. I breathe the fetid air into my lungs. Josephine was right, I think, I am absorbing this place, can't help but draw it into myself. I am surrounded by the decisions made by these people, decisions in which I've played no part. Or seem to have played no part, but even that is an illusion.

All in this dimension is an illusion, isn't that what the Buddha said? This dull sky . . . this dirty river . . . this clogged street . . . these harried people . . . I, myself . . . not really existing, could that be right?

I am running, running to free myself from this pain, from the limitations of my fear, running to put my mind at ease, in order. Thoughts bubble up from the depths, clearing a path through the confusion in my mind. Old snatches of prayers, words of wisdom, something to hang on to: Make me a channel of your peace, I plead; Faith can move mountains, I will move mountains, to bring you to me; We are all one, there is nothing that exists that is not yours.

Beautiful words, words of comfort. One of my favorite poems comes, whole and shining, a Rilke poem that I memorized during another searing experience, long ago.

Whom will you cry to, heart? More and more lonely,
your path struggles on through incomprehensible
mankind. All the more futile perhaps
for keeping to its direction,
keeping on toward the future,
toward what has been lost.

Once. You lamented? What was it? A fallen berry
of jubilation, unripe.

But now the whole tree of my jubilation
is breaking, in the storm it is breaking, my slow
tree of joy.
Loveliest in my invisible
landscape, you that made me more known
to the invisible angels.

I run for miles with the Rilke poem. He understood so completely. My slow tree of joy is breaking, my fallen berry of jubilation, unripe. My pain starts to ebb in the flow of his words, in the camaraderie of his voice. I wonder about the invisible angels, what do they do? Perhaps love attracts them, like moths to a flame. If that is true, then they must be around me now.

With that thought I feel a chill run the length of my body, the breath of angels rippling across my skin. I slow down, stop running, there is nothing to run from, and nothing to run to. I will just float on the waves of life for a while, and see what happens.

After my run, I sit in the café in the hotel lobby, drinking tea, writing in my journal, thinking. Why did I feel such a profound sense of grief? What did I lose? Nothing, really. I came to China for an adventure, and for two days I thought I might bring home a baby. For two days my world changed, and I embraced that change, and now my arms are empty.

The Indian sage Krishnamurti says that fear is the gap between the known and the unknown. Moving from one to the other causes so much fear to arise that the chasm is hardly ever crossed. If what is known is unhappiness, grief, and despair, then happiness, joy, and life will be the unknown. This situation has been so unexpected, has happened so suddenly, that I have been catapulted across the gap, fear never had a chance to take hold.

Now I am on the other side and have taken a few steps down the road of happiness; I realize I cannot turn back. It seems that what I thought in the past was happiness was just a lesser form of anxiety, not truly freedom from it. I have to be done with the discontent, the depression, forever. I have to give up my old crutches and start walking forward toward life in every moment, no matter what happens with Baby.

Wasted time, years of it, given to sadness, questioning, fear. I must have made a choice, somewhere deep and subterranean, that I would allow the move to true happiness, that I would allow it now. Why had that happiness never occurred before now? We choose, we choose and then events confirm; events confirm and we choose again, a never ending process of creating our realities. Eventually those choices form a pattern of a life, and that pattern exerts an irresistible force upon all subsequent choices. It becomes more and more difficult to make a true change. And yet, it can be done. I have just lived it.

And now, what does this all mean? I am in uncharted territory, on my little road of happiness . . . a traveler without a map. But I think of Josephine, and I know that I must talk to her again, that she will help me understand this. I go to the phone booth off the central lobby, dial her number, and she is there in a moment, on the other end of the line. I tell her what has happened, that Alex has changed her mind again and wants to keep Baby, that I was overwhelmed with grief, but that I am finding peace somehow.

"It was absolutely the right thing," she says, "to step away. I have been in prayer almost constantly since your last call. I can't tell you everything now, it's better if I wait until you are back safely. But I need to ask you, have you done any prayers or meditation since we spoke last?"

"Yes," I tell her. "I was meditating last night and I saw the most extraordinary thing. The Virgin Mary came to me, my mother was there too."

"What happened, what did she do?" Josephine asks.

"Well, she handed me the baby," I say.

Josephine sits in silence on the other end for a moment. And then she says, "I don't know how to tell you this."

"Just tell me."

"That is your baby. That vision is telling you that you are meant to have her," she says.

The invisible angels are back, I feel a chill ripple my skin.

"I know," I say. I know.

I already know.

*

When I finish talking with Josephine, I walk back out onto the bustling street outside the hotel. I am seeing it for the first time. I have been so distracted by the events unfolding in our little world that I have not really looked, not really seen. Now it comes into focus. I breathe the air, feel the vibrations of life around me. I look into people's faces, and what I perceived before as a vaguely hostile attitude now appears to be an attractive seriousness, a dignity. A small woman carrying a large wicker basket nods, and smiles shyly. A young mother holds her little boy over the curb as he urinates from the split pants that are worn by babies in China, and she laughs. A young man dressed in a neatly pressed white shirt and pleated trousers opens a door for me, and bows slightly.

I enter a small grocery store around the corner from the hotel. Walking up and down the aisles is a revelation. Bright, colorful packages with mysterious contents, unusual fruits wrapped in tissue paper, personal products for Asian skin and hair (no Cindy Crawford here). In the cookie aisle, I spend half an hour studying the different boxes and bags, curious about what might be inside, which ones would Baby like? Everything is exotic, fresh, exciting.

I tote my basket to the checkout line, and lay the merchandise I have selected on the counter: an apple, a banana, two small plastic bowls with pictures of Chinese children playing, two boxes of cookies, a bag of powdered baby formula, an orange drink. A young woman works the antiquated cash register, says something to me in Chinese, and I shake my head to indicate my lack of understanding. She points to the numbers displayed through the window of the register, the number of yuan the products cost. I hold out a small roll of paper yuan; she looks through the bills and selects two, and some coins. I thank her, having no idea if she took the correct amount, and not caring. I leave the store, eating my apple, feeling the breeze on my face, enjoying a sense of ease and well-being, feeling like myself for the first time since this trip began. What has changed in me has brought a new world to my sight; love has grown and now determines how I see.

I return to the hotel just in time to shower and change clothes before we leave for the airport for our flight to Guangzhou. Alex is on the floor with Baby on her lap, reading through a stack of official papers she will have to submit at the U.S. consulate tomorrow. Baby is trying to play, to engage Alex's attention, and Alex sighs, shifts her weight, tries to avoid the baby's waving hands. Every now and then as I move about the room, Baby and

I make eye contact, and I send her a silent, surreptitious greeting. . . . Hello, Baby. Everything is going to be okay, Baby.

We drag our luggage to the lobby, and load it into the van, and again the three families and Anna climb aboard. Traveling from Beijing to Nanchang did not seem arduous, but now we have the babies. Strollers, blankets, diaper bags, food and bottles, in addition to the huge pieces of luggage, must be negotiated through the airport check-in. Passports and tickets are being checked two and three times, while babies fuss and cry.

Waiting in the gate area, Alex keeps sighing, deep heavy exhalations of breath, as she shifts Baby from one hip to the other, or walks around the orange plastic seats. She seems annoyed, but I attribute this to the frustration of traveling. I am feeling strangely elated, talking with the others in the group, playing word games with Maggie.

Free of turmoil, and free of projecting disaster or paradise scenarios into the future, I can enjoy exactly where I happen to be, which is in an airport in China, with a group of people in the midst of an amazing journey. I think back to when I first met Judy, Curtis, Louise, and Jimmy, at the adoption agency six weeks ago. Alex had asked me to attend the meeting, as it was to go over details about the trip, and we chatted in her car on the drive into D.C.

"So, how are you feeling about the adoption? Are you getting excited?" I asked her.

"Yes . . ." she answered, her voice trailing off. "But nervous, too. There's been so much to think about, with the paperwork and the trip to plan for. Sometimes I forget there's a baby involved!"

I laughed, but then her tone turned serious. "You know, no one in my family thinks this is a good idea."

"Really? Why not?" I asked, incredulous. "Like who?"

"Well, my mom and my sister are totally against it."

"Sherrie doesn't think it's a good idea?" Sherrie is her sister, whom I know slightly. I had recently been running into Sherrie at the strangest times and places, but she never mentioned being opposed to the adoption.

"She and my mom think I should just leave well enough alone. I have my son, and that should be enough, they think."

How odd this sounds, I thought, but kept it to myself as we arrived at the agency and Alex became distracted with organizing the briefcases and files for the adoption.

We found the room designated for the meeting, the others who would be traveling with us to China already seated at the table inside. Louise and Jimmy were experienced hands at this adoption process. They were returning for their second child, and knew the ropes.

"There's no heat in the government buildings; be prepared to be cold!" warned Jimmy as he mock-shivered. Louise added that we didn't need to bring a lot of clothes, as the Chinese laundry in each of the hotels was very good, and cheap. They bubbled over with information, talking over each other in their haste to let us know each vital piece of information. I started trying to write things down: "umbrella/slicker"; "Beijing cold, Hong Kong warm"; "apply for visa after itinerary set"; "long underwear"; "gifts from U.S.—hats, nail polish, sports memorabilia"; but finally couldn't keep up. Alex asked a lot of questions, but as I watched her, it occurred to me that she really wasn't interested; the questions were an attempt to keep the social ball rolling, and something to hide behind. She wrote nothing down.

Judy and Curtis sat at the end of the table a little away from the others. I began talking with them, introducing myself as Alex's traveling companion and not an adopting parent. I asked them about their decision to adopt.

"We've thought about this for a very long time," offered Judy. "And then the process has been so long and grueling. We just want to get the trip over with," she said, as the social worker from the agency appeared and greeted everyone, handing out fresh packets of information to add to the growing stack.

"Read these carefully," she intoned. "You don't want to be in China and have a problem. Especially make sure you get all your vaccinations, and take antibiotics with you. The last thing you want to do is end up in a hospital in China."

All these warnings were not very reassuring. I looked through the papers as she continued with details about the trip, and several passages jumped out at me: "give half a teaspoon of Benadryl every six hours if on return flight child is incon-solable," "Nix cream for lice recommended," "donation to or-phanage required—$3,000 U.S.," "married but traveling without spouse must provide forms I-600A and form I-864 with notarized power of attorney authenticated by State De-partment and Chinese embassy."

With this one meeting I was on information overload, and I wondered how these prospective parents must feel. After the meeting was over and we were riding home in the car, I asked Alex how she and the others handled the stress.

"By not thinking about it," she replied. "You just do what you have to do to get through."

My mind immediately slipped into therapist mode, trying to gauge what this could mean. How could that be possible, to not think about the emotions, and the larger meanings of all this? And adoption . . . having a child, one of the most monumental undertakings in life, no matter how it comes about. And she was trying not to think about it. I decided to challenge this position, introduce something that might shift her out of automatic pilot.

"You know, I have a friend who is a mystic. Her name is Josephine, she and I talk once a week or so about various things. I was telling her about this trip the other day, and she told me that when people adopt, they are adopting exactly the right child, there are no mistakes."

"Really?" she said, shooting her eyes sideways at me, an invitation to go ahead. "I hope she's right."

"Yes; she says it's a metaphysical thing, they are drawn together by past karma. It's really interesting . . . and you know what? I've been having so many dreams about China and about this trip, and about the baby you are going to get. All these dreams are so emotional, I feel this is going to be very intense. Are you ready for that?" I queried, not sure if I'd gone too far.

She was quiet for a moment and then turned to look right into my eyes.

"Why do you think I asked you to come?"

∽

The stewardess for China Air calls our flight number, and we move toward the boarding gate with the other passengers, a mass of businessmen dressed in identical dark blue suits, pressing in close, pushing toward the gateway. All the seats on the flight are assigned, so it's unclear what the rush is. We squeeze ourselves onto the plane, find our row, and sit three across. Alex is in the window seat with Baby on her lap, I take the middle seat, and Anna sits next to me.

During the short flight, Anna and I talk. I ask her about her family, her job. She tells me that she has a husband and a young daughter, six years old. She studied at the University of Beijing, and earned the equivalent of a master's degree there. I ask her if she would like to visit America, and she says yes, she would; but it is difficult to obtain a visa, and she thinks she may never get the chance to go.

I tell Anna that I think all the men in China look mean. She wrinkles up her nose, and squints her eyes. "You do?" she asks. Yes, I say, they all have such stern expressions; I hardly ever see a man smile here. Anna tells me that no, they are not mean; they just don't show any deference to women, it's the way things are in China.

Anna struggles against her natural shyness and ventures a question: "Do all American men beat their wives?" she asks, almost apologetically. Now it is my turn to wrinkle my nose and squint my eyes in surprise.

"No!" I laugh. "Where did you get that?" She says that this is what they are told in China; that all American men beat their wives. I want to ask exactly who it is who tells them that, but don't. Instead I say, "That's news to me. I wouldn't be married to one if they did!" We giggle together then; Anna covers her mouth with her hand, like a little girl who has just said something naughty.

During the flight Alex sits with her head slightly turned, looking out the window at a bank of clouds. Baby keeps trying to get my attention, touches my hand, leans over to try to get into my lap. No, Baby, I say silently. I'm sorry, Baby, but I can't pick you up.

I want so badly to reach over and grab her, pull her to me. But I know that if Alex senses any sort of longing in me for the baby that it will interfere with her emotional process in deciding about the adoption. Josephine and I had talked about how there was almost a perversion in the way that Alex handed Baby out to me, and then so casually pulled her back, at worst toying deliberately with my emotions, at best showing a crass insensitivity.

Until now I have been inclined to give Alex the benefit of the doubt, to be understanding about her emotional turmoil concerning the baby. Josephine, however, introduced an idea I had not considered, that Alex is doing this deliberately, that she is being cruel. "But why?" I asked Josephine. "Why in the world would she do that?" Josephine didn't answer, and I knew that she was holding something back, something she had seen in her meditation or prayer work and was not willing to tell me now.

And then I thought of something Alex had said, the night she told me she couldn't take the baby. She told me that she was jealous of how attached the baby had become to me in those first two days. I protested then, told Alex that it was natural for the baby to become attached to me; I was the one caring for her, in this strange and frightening new situation. And I pointed out to her that it had been she herself who had kept her distance from the baby, that the baby had not rejected her. But then she said that what she was jealous of was my happiness with the baby, my feelings for the baby, because she did not feel that way.

My antenna had gone up then, it had seemed so irrational. What was really going on here? And when Josephine told me of her suspicions about Alex's true motives, I remembered the hard look on Alex's face when she had talked of her jealousy, the cold tone of her voice. It may be true, I thought, that Alex is being deliberately cruel, but I have to hold to the one thought that seems of the highest order, and not be distracted; and that one thought is for the happiness and well-being of Baby.

How could she not fall completely in love with Baby, I keep thinking, over and over as I watch the two of them together. Baby is sitting on Alex's lap facing her, reaching her hands out in front to try to play with the buttons on Alex's shirt. Alex reaches up without looking at Baby, and moves her little hands away.

Please love her, I keep thinking, if you are going to take her, please love her. And yet a part of me feels that she should not have her, that her love for Baby would always be imperfect, a house built upon a shaky foundation.

I lean back against the seat and close my eyes. It is nighttime now, the sky beyond the window black, the lights on inside the cabin. Suddenly I am very, very tired, and I want to sleep, but cannot. I lost something that I never had. I am missing something I had not even known that I wanted. What should I do now? Start my own adoption proceedings, come back to China and get a little girl of my own? But it is this little girl, this one. . . . And even though I know that what Josephine said is true, this baby is meant to be mine, for reasons I don't understand—even though I feel so strongly Baby belongs with me—Alex is the one who meant to adopt her, and I have no power to make her mine.

There was a dream last night, something about helping a Chinese emperor to make an important decision? I try to grab on to pieces that float by in my mind: something about a bird flying off into the sky . . . the Emperor . . . trying to find the right words to say to him, it seemed of utmost importance . . . and then it is there, the whole of the dream reconstructed, and I let myself drift into the scene:

I spent many nights after our marriage talking with the Emperor on any number of subjects. He would summon me to

*his chambers, where an elaborate meal had been prepared, and
we would eat together as we talked, sometimes until dawn. He
was becoming increasingly alarmed at the continued uprisings
in the land—they seemed to be spreading and without any single cause. Our talks together comforted him, and he would
leave in the morning with a softer countenance, after kissing me
chastely upon the cheek each time.*

*When he left I would return to the courtyard of my cham-
bers, where Chen would be waiting with a bird on each arm.
From his waist hung a small leather pouch and I would untie
the pouch from his belt, and place into it a jewel that I happened to be wearing, an emerald, diamond, or pearl, sometimes
sapphire or gold, and I would pull the string tight before affix-
ing the pouch to the fragile leg of the bird.*

*Chen would then lift his arm and set the birds free to fly out-
side the palace walls, to a place where Chen had trained them to
go, to a place where the jewels might be used to lift those in need,
where they might be exchanged for food or shelter or clothing. I
watched the birds take wing and each time my mind soared
with the birds, to the countryside where the villages lay in quiet
humility, where those who suffered did so quietly. And I prayed
that the sky open to receive this offering and shelter the birds
throughout their journey. Not one bird thus sent failed to return,
the empty pouch dangling freely, the offering accepted.*

*One evening I was summoned to the Emperor's chamber,
and it was clear as I entered the room that he suffered from deep
agitation. I felt almost pity for him, so evident was his discomfort. He asked me to sit before him, and I did, the silk of my skirt
billowing around me to create a quiet pool in which I floated,
listening to his words, absorbing his meaning, letting compassion bathe my awareness. The Emperor told me he was leaving,*

that he must travel far into the countryside where there was a fe-
rocious battle being waged, a battle that could determine
whether or not his rule would continue in that province, or be
overthrown. If the peasants there took control, there was a possi-
bility of other neighboring provinces banding together to do like-
wise, and the Emperor himself was needed to quell this uprising
at any cost, to spur his wearied troops to unqualified victory.

The Emperor poured out his heart to me. He told me of his
distaste for battle, of his fear of the final outcome. This fear was
palpable; it hung in the room and reminded me of the black
cloud I had seen the day in the temple, when I had collapsed
from its weight. And yet now it did not disturb me, I could feel
my strength in relation to it had grown, that its only power was
over the weak. I remembered my vow to love the Emperor, and
thought that this is what it meant: to seek to encourage and
nurture his own strength in relation to this dark cloud of fear,
to show him of its powerlessness over one who chooses love.

When the Emperor finished speaking, we sat for some mo-
ments in silence. In time a question arose in me, a question
whose answer had the power to change that fear into good. "It
is possible to be free of fear, to have complete victory over it." I
spoke slowly, deliberately. "And yet that victory is never simply
given. It must be chosen. Tell me: Do you desire such a victory?"

The Emperor sat in his abject misery, and when he turned
his head from me, I knew that the question had not reached
him. "I desire victory over those who seek to overthrow me!" he
said with vehemence. "I must defend myself and my lands,
those things bequeathed to me through the imperial lineage. If I
lose any part of that which I was given, I have failed!"

Quickly my response came, "On the contrary, it is that
which you have simply accepted from others that will burden

you utmost! You must choose for yourself, for choice is our only true power."

His anger rose then. "And what of this uprising, shall I just allow it to occur?" His eyes blazed with indignation.

"Sir, it is victory over the self that is the only true victory! You may defeat this uprising, but what of the next? Will you live in fear, will you choose to be a slave to those whom you rule?" I said with a force of conviction that stunned the Emperor into silence.

The Emperor nodded, though he did not understand. "Help me, Empress; help me to see," he said in this unguarded moment, when his fear was greater than his pride.

"How? How can I help you?" I asked gently.

He reached for my hands then, and spoke hesitantly, not used to asking, used only to dictating his desires to those who could not refuse. "Write to me while I am away. Tell me of things that you know. I shall be away some months, and when I return, perhaps you and I may . . . perhaps our duty to the empire shall be fulfilled at last!"

I promised him that I would do so, and bade him good-bye. That night as I lay in my own bed, my union with the Emperor as yet unconsummated, I felt the stirrings of life within my womb, and I accepted that life, and prayed for its protection. But not for my own.

I feel a strange sensation of falling; did I fall asleep, or am I just remembering that dream? I shiver and open my eyes. Alex is looking at me, looking right into my eyes.

"It's happening again," she says.

I am confused, disoriented. "What?" I say.

"The panic. I'm feeling panicked, like I have to get away

from her," she says, desperation in her voice. She is holding Baby away from her body, at arm's length on her knees, as if pulling her close would be painful.

I look at them in silence. What does she mean? I thought everything was going okay; Alex seemed fine with the baby today.

"I can't do it. I really can't. I know that for sure now," she says. "I can't take her; but I can't leave her here, what will people say?"

And when she says this, I realize that I knew this would happen, deep down I knew.

"What do you want to do?" I ask her, the question vibrating in the air between us, resonating with a power that comes through me as I ask it. The power is from a source beyond me, a source that is now calling for her answer, the answer.

"I want you to take her."

There. It is done. Alex has spoken it three times, three times has denied this child. Baby is not her child, could never be her child.

She is mine.

∽

Guangzhou is a far different type of city than Nanchang or Beijing. It is warm, semitropical, with neon lights, commerce, Western-style buildings. Even at ten o'clock at night the city is bustling, traffic clogging the roads. During the ride from the airport I watch eagerly through the window as the city unfolds. Signs for McDonald's, Motorola, Sony, even Starbucks, line the streets, and something in my gut unclenches, a recognition that we have returned to civilization.

The van pulls up in front of a very large building, the luxurious White Swan Hotel complex, which is connected with the U.S. consulate. The hotel is famous, having been used over the years as a showcase for powerful Western visitors. Richard Nixon, among others, stayed here, and the service is geared toward satisfying the discerning traveler. In the last few years the White Swan has become famous as the hotel in which every American who adopts from China stays while awaiting their visa from the consulate, and in adoption circles it has been jokingly renamed "The White Stork." The hotel is technically on an island, separated from the rest of the city by a ring of water, but joined to it by footbridges and pedestrian walkways.

Anna tells the parents that they have to take the babies to have their pictures taken for the visa application, and it must be done tonight, immediately, so they are ready for the appointment tomorrow morning at the consulate. Everyone is tired, there is grumbling about this; but there is no way to avoid it, it must be done.

Alex and I stay in the van for a moment to talk after everyone gets out.

"Do you want me to take Baby for her picture?" I ask.

"No, you'd better not," she answers. "I don't want anyone to start asking questions."

I agree, and Alex takes Baby and puts her in the stroller for the short walk to where the picture will be taken. I go inside and check into the hotel and find our room, a lovely room with a dramatic view of the churning Pearl River below. Even now, after ten p.m., barges travel the waters here in this busy port city, and I watch as their hulking silhouettes move past in the darkness.

Now that I have a few quiet minutes to myself, I think about calling my husband. He doesn't even know about Alex's change of mind this morning, or her abrupt reversal tonight. He has no idea of the emotional turmoil of these past few hours, and I feel the need to talk to someone, confide in someone, be comforted by someone.

When he answers the phone I can hear in his voice a distance that was not there last night, a businesslike attitude that catches me off guard. His many years of working in the political environment of Capitol Hill have taught him to detach his emotions from the task at hand, and he has honed this skill to perfection. It's not the time for that, I think; where is the man from the phone call of last night, the one who said with a sob in his voice, "Bring her home"? I immediately sink into the exhaustion I have been fighting, an exhaustion that has taken an entire lifetime to build.

He says, in his brisk Washington way, that he and Alex's husband had a meeting with an attorney earlier today, that they discussed the situation, and that the lawyer gave them some strong advice, which my husband thinks we should heed. "He says we can't do it. There is no way we can adopt this child."

The exhaustion. I can't answer him, so suddenly has it come upon me and doused my spirit. The exhaustion of dreams denied, always denied. Mindless practicalities always seem to get the upper hand over beautiful but unrealistic visions. Just once, I would like to see it go the other way.

"Hello?" he says, not sure I am still on the line.

I have to pull energy from somewhere to speak, and finally I do. "Why not?" I ask, with no anger or emotion at all in my voice. I hear the flat tone and think, I will never be the same.

"He said we may run into trouble with immigration. If Alex goes through with the adoption in China, knowing she is not going to keep the baby, the INS could charge her with fraud. For us to try to adopt the baby after you get back here would be a red flag—they might think it was planned."

Planned! It is so absurd. Why would I have someone else adopt a baby for me?

"The lawyer was absolutely adamant that we should not try to do this. If the INS were to go after Alex for fraud, she could go to jail. We can't put her in that position, I won't do it. I don't see any way we can do this," he says, with finality.

"No, we can't put Alex in that position, I agree. But what about the baby?" I ask. Why does everyone keep forgetting about her?

He continues talking, about the regulations, the INS restrictions, legal opinions, and reasons why it can't be done. My mind rejects every word he says—I don't even listen to the details. I know with every cell of my body that Baby will be mine.

"There has to be a way," I say, ignoring his certainty that this is impossible. There is always a way.

"Look, I know you really want this, and I'm sorry, but it's not going to happen. Your emotions are clouding your thinking right now, I understand that. But I'm telling you, we can't adopt her, and that's just the way it is."

Now I am angry. "That's the way it is" just is not going to cut it here. I am angry at him, angry that he accepts this verdict so easily. I say, "I have never thought so clearly in all my life," and I have not. I tell him that the only cloudy thinking is the lawyer's, and his, and that he doesn't understand what is happening here. For all the lip service people give to valuing human life, when the chips are down, regulations must be followed.

"There has to be a way. There has to be someone else you can call, someone who can help us. I refuse to give up based on one person's opinion. This is too important. I won't rest until we've exhausted all the possibilities, every one of them," I say, my voice rising in defiance.

"I have been afraid of this, that you would get your hopes up, start thinking this was going to happen, and then it doesn't work and you are disappointed. You have to know the odds are not good on this, you have to know it's not likely," he says.

It may not be likely, I think, but unlikely things happen all the time, all the time. The odds are against people winning the lottery, too, and yet people do. Wouldn't the odds be better if we didn't give up, if we explored all possibilities? It seems so obvious to me, how can he not see this?

"I know that, I know! Alex already changed her mind today, twice! Do you think I'm not aware how many obstacles there are? It's excruciating, but what should I do, give up? I can't do that, I would never forgive myself, never," I say.

He is silent for a moment. Then he says he will think about what to do next; he is at least going to reconsider the idea that this is impossible. I tell him I will call him again tomorrow, and just as I am hanging up the phone, Alex walks into the room with Baby, and I tell her about what my husband said. She immediately wants to call her husband. She is concerned, now that she has made up her mind, and she does not want anything to interrupt her plan. "I want to hear what that lawyer had to say for myself," she says, and starts trying to place the call.

I take Baby from her and start dressing her for bed. It feels so good to hold her again. I take off the pink dress that is too big; I stick her arms and legs into the one-piece sleeper suit that has little pictures of lipsticks, hairbrushes, compacts, and purses on it. Cosmetics on a baby sleeper, why? I look at the label; it reads MADE IN CHINA. Isn't everything? They are exporting everything, including their unwanted girl babies.

Baby has her bottle and her blanket, and I take her out to the hallway to walk until she falls asleep. The hotel floor has two hostesses to attend to the guests' every need, and as soon as we open the door they approach us and coo over the baby. One of the hostesses says that she sees a lot of Americans here adopting Chinese babies. "You like her?" she asks hopefully, indicating Baby.

"Yes, I like her; I like her very much," I say.

"She have good life," the hostess says. Yes.

Around the hallway we go. The baby falls asleep easily tonight, and I take her back to the room and tuck her into the wooden crib next to the bed. I did not notice when we first arrived, but the room has one king-size bed, instead of two smaller beds, and Alex and I will have to share it tonight. Alex is still on the phone, asking her husband pointed questions about the meeting with the lawyer, her voice rising as she demands answers.

"That's ridiculous!" I hear her exclaim, as I head out the door in my running shoes, looking for the hotel gym, somewhere I can clear my head. The hotel is huge. I wander through a labyrinth of hallways, through the lobby, following the signs to an outside terrace to the entrance of the glass-walled gymnasium. There is an attendant at the door; he hands me a towel and leads me inside. There are only two other people here working out, as it is late. I choose a treadmill in the far corner and get on, start to walk. The treadmill is set directly in front of the full-length glass wall, and I can see the dark river beyond the window, the lights on the barges, which are strung like Christmas trees, moving slowly up and down the waterway.

I can also see my reflection in the glass, superimposed over the image of the river beyond. The effect is that in the image, it looks as if I am walking on the water. A barge goes by, and I am walking on its deck. It passes and I walk on the water again. The treadmill speeds up, now I am running, and always when I run, emotions lodged deep in my tissues start to release, to ripple up to my chest. My chest becomes tight, my heart constricts, warmth spreading up to my shoulders and neck.

Grief. Again, for a short time, I thought Baby would be mine. Again, a major obstacle arises, and I am thrown back on myself. A test . . . a test of what, my strength? Stamina? I don't know, I don't know. You never get what you want, so don't want anything precious. I should not have wanted, should not have wanted. I am so tired, so tired and I'll never be the same.

I am sobbing and I'm glad no one can see me, that I am facing only myself, my reflection in the glass. And there, I am walking on water.

~

When I have pulled myself together, when I am finished with my run, I go to the hotel business center, where I can borrow a computer and send an e-mail. I need to reach out, to communicate with someone; tonight it has hit me how alone and isolated I am here, on the other side of the world from home. I don't feel I can speak on the telephone with this heavy burden of despair weighing on my chest, but connecting to something familiar and known seems like a healthy impulse; I sit down at a terminal and log on to the Internet, and find waiting for me a message from Josephine:

> Don't forget that nothing is as it appears to be. Time is not linear. Do not allow Alex to torture you. If you must, and no matter how hard it may be, just hand the baby back to her; call her bluff. All will work out, there is soul group activity in action that will assist you along the way.
>
> Love and Light,
> Josephine

She is trying to comfort me, but tonight I cannot be comforted. I am deep inside myself, I cannot see my way out. Disappointment and discouragement pushed below the surface in other times are swirling around me, pulling me under, and it seems that the most cherished of my dreams never, ever come true. All the world's teachings seem inadequate in this moment, in the face of these feelings. "Do not allow Alex to torture you. . . ." How can she torture me any more than I torture myself? I try to come up with words that do not betray my anguish, for that in itself is a failure on my part, a failure of faith.

Josephine,

    This has been the strangest day of my life. We flew to Guangzhou tonight, and during the flight Alex told me once again that she can't take this baby; I was elated, then called my husband and he told me there was no way for us to adopt her due to INS regulations, etc. I am so tired now. Just wanted to fill you in on the latest, I have no idea how this is all going to end. We leave for Hong Kong tomorrow afternoon, will call you from there. Please have words of wisdom ready. . . .

I sign off, and go back to our room. Alex has put Baby to sleep in the crib in the corner of the room, so she whispers as she fills me in on her conversation with her husband. The lawyer they met with is a family friend, and is very concerned about the INS charging her with fraud. Apparently he has suggested that if Alex goes through with the adoption in China, and brings Baby back to the United States with the intention of giving her up to us, then the best thing to do would be to relinquish Baby upon arrival.

"Relinquish her to whom?" I ask.

"He said he could arrange for a Social Services representative to come and get the baby at the airport when we arrive, and have her placed immediately into foster care. And that's not all; he thinks it would be better to place her in another state altogether, like New York."

"What? Take her to New York? But why? Why not just place her with us as foster parents right off the bat? We already know we want to adopt her," I say.

"He said that if we placed her in another state, the courts would not suspect that this was planned in some way. There might be a better chance for you to adopt her," Alex says, as if this makes perfect sense.

This is insanity. The thought of handing Baby over to a stranger at the airport, having her taken somewhere away from us, makes my stomach turn. We cannot do that to her, not after all she has been through.

"No," I say to Alex. "No, we can't do that."

"But it may be the only way for you to adopt her! And I can't leave her here now, in China; we've come too far. So there has to be a plan for when we get back."

So, she has decided not to leave her here; at least we have that. And though I know from comments she has made that she is doing this not for Baby, but to save herself from a life of guilt, I am still grateful and relieved and happy for Baby.

"Well, I'll go to New York with her then, or wherever I have to go. I'll stay with her until I can bring her home," I say.

"You will? You would do that?" Alex asks, incredulous.

Of course I would. I'll do whatever it takes; I have resigned myself to that. I will not leave her to face a strange situation alone again, not if I can help it. "I still believe there's a way, an easier way. I just feel it," I say. Alex looks at me and nods, and we fall silent.

We pick at our room service trays, but don't really eat. Neither one of us has eaten much these last five days, and the stress is starting to show. Alex looks gaunt, her face drawn. She has lost weight, though she was already thin to begin with; she hasn't slept much. At least I have been sleeping, even though it is fitful sleep and full of exhausting dreams.

"I've got to try to sleep," she says, and we get into the big bed. There is a vast unbridgeable distance between us, we cannot comfort each other. Alex rolls to her side, and I to mine, each alone with our private anguish. I try to sleep, but this night it is I who cannot surrender. I imagine Baby, now sleeping peacefully in her crib in the corner, being pulled away from me at the airport, her terror and shock. I try to imagine her being adopted by another family, somewhere in New York.

I want what is best for her, only what is best. I cannot even picture her with someone else, what is best for her is to come home with me! No, I won't allow this craziness! I sit bolt upright in bed. Alex is snoring softly, finally finding refuge in sleep. The baby breathes in her crib, and I look at the clock; it is well past midnight, I have been tossing for an hour.

I get out of bed and peek into the crib at Baby before going to the bathroom. There is a telephone there, in a little private room where the toilet is. I go in and close the door, sit on the commode, trying to be as quiet as I can be. I dial my husband's number at work, he should be there now, it is afternoon where he is.

While I wait for him to come to the phone, I think, How did this happen, how? I feel caught in a dream, one I can't wake up from, a dream that gets more and more bizarre each moment.

He comes on the line, surprised that I have called again so soon. I tell him I can't sleep, I have been turning this over and over in my mind, and that I just cannot accept this, can't accept that there's not another way.

He begins telling me that I need to understand, we cannot adopt this baby.

"No, no! I don't want to hear that, I won't listen to that. I just don't believe it. I know there is some way, we just need to call the right person, the person who can help us," I say, trying to keep my voice low but having trouble doing so, there is too much emotion.

"There is no one to call," he says sadly. "This guy is an immigration attorney, he knows what he's talking about."

"I don't care who he is! I don't believe it, it makes no sense. This is wrong, wrong. . . . All we want to do is bring home a baby that nobody else wanted! Nobody wanted her, not even Alex! And now, because of some ludicrous regulations, some idiot lawyer's opinion, she can't be with us, she can't have a home?"

"It makes no sense, but that's the way it is," he says, trying to keep his own voice low, so others in the office don't overhear.

"I don't accept the way it is! I can't!" I am crying now, loud sobs, I can't hold it back any longer. "Don't you understand? This is life and death, hers and mine. I can't explain this, but if we can't adopt her, I'll never be the same! I've never felt this way before, about anything; I've never wanted anything so much! I don't know why, I just love this baby so much, so much it hurts. I just love her!"

He listens, not offering platitudes or empty words of comfort, and that is a relief. Finally, he says that he will think about what to do, that he will do what he can. "That's all I ask," I say. "Do what you can."

I hang up, and go to the sink, where I splash cold water on my face. I look in the mirror, my eyes are red, my face white. I am scoured out, empty, depleted, weak. Alex is still sleeping when I get back into bed—she hasn't heard a thing; nor has Baby, who lies motionless in her crib.

I am dying, and they are sound asleep. I pull the sheet and blanket up around me, huddling inside, and wrap my arms around my knees, pulling them to my chest. A womb, a cocoon; in this muffled darkness I let go, give in to the tide of feelings breaking free. A roiling, thunderous surf pounds in my ears, my gut is heaving with painful contractions. My cries come from too deep a place to even make a sound.

Why, why, why? Why do I feel this way? A baby I met only two days ago, and my love for her could crack me in two. I would turn the world upside down and heaven inside out if it would bring her to me. Where did these feelings come from? The embers of my heart have been covered with ashes for so long, and now they have become a roaring flame.

I must let it consume me now, I cannot fight this conflagration. May it burn all dross from my being; let the blaze temper my will. My will, yes, my will . . . what do I will?

> *The human Will, that force unseen,*
> *The offspring of a deathless Soul,*
> *Can hew the way to any goal,*
> *Though walls of granite intervene.*

This poem springs to life in my mind . . . it is one that I have long admired. The title of the poem is "Will," but I never truly understood it until this moment. What if that is true? What if, just what if, a decision I make, a steeling of my will, can hew the way to any goal? What if faith can move mountains? And what if the greatest force is love?

In the deep lucidity of my pain, I see that I have never lived any of these truths, ever. My life has had no real power.

And with this realization, I let it all go rushing out from me, a tidal wave of desire, love, faith, passion, longing; it rolls out into every corner of the universe, to anywhere in any time where God might exist. From this moment of release forward, I am no longer myself alone, but part of that force unseen, which is life. Someday soon, the cocoon will break open, and I will be free.

Be not impatient in delay,
But wait as one who understands;
When spirit rises and commands,
The gods are ready to obey.

Sleep comes over me like a blessing, to heal my battered soul.

this place," and with that I stopped, as a look of realization dawned on Shiu Lin's face, and she began to weep.

"Oh, Mistress, this cannot be! No, tell me it is not so! For when the Emperor finds out, I cannot think of what will happen, what will happen to us all!" she wailed, sobbing uncontrollably, her head in my lap.

I sat calmly, stroking her hair. "That is why no one must know."

"But how? How can this be kept secret?" she asked through her sobs.

"The Emperor will be away a great while, Shiu Lin. It may be possible, but I will need your help!" I exclaimed, holding her face between my hands, wiping her tears.

"Of course, I will do anything, Mistress, anything at all!" she cried, sitting up and collecting herself at last. "I will tell Madam immediately, she will help us too. Oh, Mistress . . . let us believe we can!"

I smiled at her in gratitude. "I believe we can, Shiu Lin, for we must save this child. But now we must seek to conceal my condition, as you saw today the evidence of it," I said, placing my hand upon the swell at my belly. "My clothing must be made to be loose and unrestrictive. We have some time to prepare our other plans."

She hugged me tightly, and left me then. I began to think of ways to tell Shiu Lin that we must think of one who could keep the child safe, once it was born to me. It must be safe outside the palace walls; it could not live within them. And I knew we must begin to pray for its protection, and find a way in our hearts to let it go.

☙

By morning, peace has descended. I wake early, a diffused light glowing through the shuttered windows. I hear the barges passing on the river below, their low rumble hypnotic and soothing. What has passed in the night, what grace has been bestowed, that I could move from agony to acceptance? I still love Baby,

Will

My court lady-in-waiting, Shiu Lin, noticed while he[ ] ing me to dress that there was a swell at my belly. I sa[ ] her eyes linger there, a quizzical look upon her face, be[ ] fore her eyes came up to mine, and were met with confirmation. "Yo[ ] are with child, Mistress?" she asked.

"Yes, Shiu Lin; I am with child," I replied, and looked past Shiu Lin's happy face to the blossoms on the rosebush, which were already fading.

Shiu Lin jumped up, clapping her hands together. "Then we must alert the palace! We must inform the Emperor, and tell the happy news that there will be a continuation of the imperial lineage," she said in delight.

"No, Shiu Lin. We must not," I answered quietly but firmly. "No one must know."

"No one must know? But . . . why not? I do not understand. . . ." Shiu Lin said, struggling to make sense of my words.

I sighed deeply, and took her hand. "Shiu Lin, there is something I must tell you. . . ." I began. Drawing her into the garden, we sat for some time as I told her of my chaste meetings with the Emperor, of our talks that went far into the night, of the kiss on the cheek before he would depart, of my return each day without having consummated our union.

Shiu Lin listened, with barely disguised impatience. "But if the marriage has not been consummated, how can you be with child?"

"There was someone else, Shiu Lin," I said. She shot me a look of disbelief, rejecting my statement immediately.

"I am with you each moment; Jiang guards our door day and night! There could be no one else!" she said.

"Shiu Lin, do you remember the morning before my wedding when I slipped away and did not return for some hours? I went to ease my heart, at Black Dragon Pool. And there I found Han, also drawn

still want her; but in that desire there is no longer any fear or need.

Alex and Baby are awake too, and we get dressed for our last day of official adoption business. The light at the end of the tunnel is visible now; after today, we will know at least one thing for sure: Baby is leaving China. The U.S. government will issue her visa this morning at the consulate, and then we are free to go home.

But first, the babies are scheduled for a medical examination. It is routine, a requirement to obtain the visa, and yet there is some anxiety about some serious malady being detected in one of the babies. The group of us walks along a brick-paved promenade in the soft morning air, looking in delight at the pastel stucco buildings that tell of Guangzhou's colonial past. It is beautiful, the buildings are from another time, another place; a little bit of Europe that somehow survived the Cultural Revolution. Schoolchildren dressed in blue-and-white uniforms perform synchronized movements on a plaza ringed with colorful flags, attractive couples stroll past arm in arm, and professionals in business suits hurry by with their briefcases tucked under their arms. A Western influence has been allowed to thrive here, and I wonder why. Why were these buildings not smashed and destroyed, along with everything else that reminded the early Communists of the decadence of capitalism and bourgeois wealth?

We reach the large modern office building that houses the medical clinic. We are ushered inside, and are asked to wait on benches outside the examining rooms. I am holding Baby, she cuddles in my arms. Today, she is wearing a bright pink sweater that makes her black eyes look even more exotic and intense than usual. We are comfortable together, she and I. She rests against me as if we've been together forever, and I breathe her in, look into her eyes. She is the most beautiful thing I've ever seen.

The babies names are called one by one, and first Judy and Curtis disappear with their baby behind a glass screen, and then Jimmy and Louise with theirs, Maggie trailing behind. And then a white-smocked attendant calls out the name that both Alex and I have been carefully avoiding using all this time, the name chosen for Baby by Alex and her husband, before this trip began. As soon as I hear it spoken, I know it was never meant for Baby, it was never right for her. It is a quintessentially American name, and would have given no hint or nod to her Asian roots. It is a label, an American label that would have been slapped over the MADE IN CHINA label that was Baby herself, in an attempt to obscure the truth.

I hand Baby to Alex and we move into an examining room. A kindly Chinese doctor is there; he speaks to us in stilted English, and indicates that Baby should be put on the table. Alex places her there and he begins gently prodding Baby's abdomen, listens to her heart, measures her head, and manipulates her arms and legs, all the while speaking a singsong Chinese, which calms Baby. It is obvious that he loves babies; he is smiling at her, maybe telling her she is beautiful, or special. Baby is enthralled; she looks up into his face and is not at all frightened, or anxious. After only a few moments and the briefest of examinations, he says, "This baby, healthy!"

I move forward, and point to marks we have noticed on her back and shoulders. "What are these?" I ask.

"Bite," he says, pinching his thumb and forefinger together, moving them up and down her back. Ah, I see; they are bug bites, from the mattress in the orphanage.

I pull Baby up to a sitting position, and indicate my concern that she can't sit up without wobbling and leaning forward. She has no muscle tone at all, no strength with which to steady herself. Her leg muscles have atrophied too. It is obvious she has not had an opportunity to move very much, if at all. Her records say she is thirteen months old, and yet she does not crawl, does not even try to roll over when placed on her back.

"Shouldn't she be able to sit?" I ask the doctor.

"No worry!" he responds, waving my question away with his hand, and leaving the room with a cheery and definitive "Good-bye!" His job is completed, another rubber stamp affixed to a cursory medical exam. But perhaps he has a special sense about this, and does know that Baby is fundamentally healthy, who knows? At least he has found nothing glaring, and there is nothing that will hold up the visa application.

We gather in the waiting room with the others. Anna comes breathlessly into the room; she tells us that we need to go quickly, "Right away!" to the U.S. consulate. Our appointment is at nine-thirty a.m. sharp, and if we are late, we may not receive the visas at all. They are very strict, she says, and will not grant another appointment should we miss this one. This sets off a panic, and we scurry outside, running down the street, strollers and diaper bags flying this way and that. We reach the heavily guarded entrance to the consulate out of breath, and with just minutes to spare. We check in with the guard and are ushered inside, past a long line of Chinese people that stretches the full length of the building. They are waiting to be given a chance to apply for a visa to visit America. They look at us with imploring eyes, envy evident on many of their faces. I feel then the privilege that it is to be an American in this world, to have the freedom to travel wherever, and whenever, we may choose.

Once inside the building, it is America. People rush about efficiently, papers in hands, glancing at watches, keeping to a schedule. Fluorescent lights illuminate tidy office cubicles, where typists click-click at full speed ahead. The hallways and offices are clean and bright, and the workers smile at us as they pass, and speak purposefully to coworkers. It is such a stark difference from the Chinese offices and government agencies we have been dealing with these past seven days—I feel as if I have stepped onto another planet. And on this planet, our appointment time is to be honored, it is not an approximation! Such a small thing, such a big relief; my nervous system locks into the rhythm of this place, this is the pace I have been wired for. I feel a sense of safety here, that we are wanted, that we belong. This feeling of safety is something I take for granted at home, in the United States, and I think of all those who have emigrated there from places like China, how alone and vulnerable they must feel, all the time.

We are shown to a waiting room that is filled with Americans adopting Chinese babies. It is cheerful chaos, books and toys scattered about, the chattering of small children, the happy murmuring of parents about to take home their new children. I play with Baby; she ignores the books and toys and instead climbs onto the back of the couch, taking every opportunity to exercise her neglected muscles. Alex goes through the trusty briefcase paperwork for the last time, pulling out thick packets of papers, rifling through in search of this piece, or that. She is nervous; what if there's a problem now?

"I don't think I could go through with the adoption if there's a big problem," she says. "I won't be able to pretend."

"There will be no problem," I say, in a low, calm voice. There can be no problem.

There is no problem. Alex is called to the desk by a young

man dressed in khakis and a button-down shirt. He has the un-threatening look of a therapist or a teacher in his first job just out of college. We sit opposite him, and he looks through the visa request and asks to see the adoption papers. Alex slides them across the desk, and he glances through them, and slides them back, no questions raised. Baby is sitting on my lap, play-ing with the buttons on my sweater, trying to put them into her mouth, oblivious to the importance of the transaction. The man asks for the Chinese passport, and Alex hands over the red-covered document, and he stamps it perfunctorily FREE TO GO.

We gather up our belongings, eager to leave the building. The relief is exquisite, we made it through! I want to dance along the sidewalk, to take Baby in my arms and swing her around. You're free, you're free! We're going to put you on a plane and take you home with us, Baby! It is a beautiful day, with warm hazy sun-shine, the palm trees sway in the breeze and we decide to take a walk through the park along the river.

We say little as we walk, but it is not an uncomfortable si-lence. We are each doing the best we can. There is a group of schoolchildren playing in the park, beautiful preadolescent girls, running and kicking a ball, laughing, the wind whipping their long black hair. Baby will look like that some day..... I stop to watch, and notice out of the corner of my eye a man standing nearby, looking at me. He might be middle-aged but it is hard to tell. His long gray beard is unkempt, and wiry hair curls from beneath a floppy brimmed hat. Is he homeless? Why is he just standing there, like he's been expecting us? He looks at me and smiles, a broad grin of invitation—"Come over, talk to me," it seems to say. I return his smile and he points to Baby. "Yours?"

I nod. "Yes; mine."

"Ahhhhhhh," he says, throwing his head back. "I knew you would be together someday."

Suddenly my vision goes dark; I see bright pricks of stars before my eyes. What? What did he say?

My vision clears and I see he is looking right into my eyes. His are dark, an indeterminate color, and they sparkle with joy. "I knew you'd be together someday," he says, again.

I just stand there, mute, mesmerized, wondering, disoriented. Did he speak those words, or did I hear them in my head? The man shuffles away, torn sandals flapping against his callused heels, still smiling his smile of secret delight.

I turn to look; Alex and the baby are a few steps away near the edge of the walkway. I want to ask her, Did you hear what that man just said? But she is looking away, toward the river, and I cannot get her attention, and I know she could not have heard.

When I look back, the man has vanished. The park is empty, the mirage of happy girls and wise old man no longer visible, but the echo of laughter lingers in the air.

∽

After our walk, we return to the hotel room. I lie on the bed, suddenly exhausted from the turmoil of the night before, the vision in the park. Baby is not tired enough to sleep so Alex offers to bathe her while I nap. She takes Baby into the bathroom and I hear the water being turned on in the tub.

Alex sticks her head around the corner into the room.

"I've been wondering, what do you think you will name her?" she asks.

Caught off guard, not expecting this question but also realizing I have not even considered a name, I lie motionless for several moments, silent. The strangeness of this, that I would be the one to give someone a name, a name that they will carry for the rest of their lives, hits me with full force. The name that Alex selected, the name that will be on all of Baby's official documents, is a name that a close family member of mine already has; we can't use this name, so another will have to be selected.

I picture Baby's face, and I think, I can't do it. She is already who she *is*, I can't "give" her a name; what name could adequately represent the fullness of her being?

"I'll have to think about it," I say, and Alex pulls her head back into the bathroom to continue attending to Baby. I think of the book I read about Chairman Mao, it mentioned that his mother never had a name; by tradition, for centuries, peasant girls in China were not important enough to be given a name, to be singled out as individuals. They were called simply "Seventh daughter of Wang" or some such designation that referred to their father, or family.

The symbolic meaning of naming Baby falls heavily upon me, and as I drift toward sleep, I pray: let the name that was meant to be hers come to me. In my dreams, let it come, so that I can give her something she can keep, forever.

⌇

As the life grew inside me, I withdrew more and more into myself. My mind and my heart centered their attention upon it and I dreamed of it each night. It was a girl child, of this I was certain. I could see her, large dark eyes shining, through the mist of my dreams. What fate awaited an orphaned girl child? My heart broke at the thought that she would live without the love of a mother, of the one who loved her beyond time. The one who loved her, I was the one who loved her. . . . Even then, before she was born, my love for her haunted me.

In the afternoon, Anna takes our group on a journey into the heart of the city's shopping district, a huge open-air market surrounded by stores and shops. To reach it, we walk along the same tree-lined boulevards we traversed this morning, and then cross a high pedestrian overpass spanning a multi-lane highway, which is clogged with traffic. Going from one side to the other is like traveling back in time; on the other side, another culture lives and thrives. The White Swan Hotel, the American consulate, and the international business community are isolated on the beautiful Shamian Island, an enclave of Western architecture and commerce. But surrounding the island is the real China, and as we descend from the walkway, we are immersed in it, surrounded by it, our own little Caucasian island in a sea of Chinese faces.

The contrast is stark. Gone are the clean-swept sidewalks, the pretty stucco villas covered in vines, the spacious plazas. In their places are narrow, broken sidewalks, gritty streets separating rows of gray or brown buildings, with laundry hanging from most of the open windows. Dirt paths, no open space, and so many people, all crowded into the confusion of the open-air market.

We stand at the entrance, uncertain, overwhelmed. Anna tells us that this is where most people do their grocery shopping, and buy clothes and household goods. Rows of colorful flags wave in the warm breeze. Signs in both English and Chinese indicate stands for vegetables, fish, pig, and rice, among other things. We move slowly forward, and I wonder about the wisdom of coming here, with the babies, when it would be so easy for one of us to get lost from the others, or step from the crumbled sidewalk and fall into the path of a rickety vehicle or into a basket of scorpions.

Anna waves us on from up ahead, "Come on!" She is a little impatient with us in our hesitancy. We try to obey her command, but we quickly fall farther behind, looking left, looking right, stopping and gawking every few feet. Glancing behind me, I see Alex pushing Baby in the stroller. On the way over she had suggested that she take charge of Baby during the group outing, as she was worried that the others were starting to become suspicious. Apparently, Jimmy had made a comment the night before that alluded to the fact that Alex never seemed to be caring for her own child.

When the group had gone to get the babies' pictures taken for their passports, leaving me behind at the hotel, he had said to Alex, "So where's her Mom?," indicating Baby, making joking reference to me. The comment unnerved her, so now she pushes Baby, looking miserable. Baby looks uncomfortable, too, sitting forward in the stroller seat, anxious eyes scanning the scene. There is so much to take in, and I wish I could be holding her, comforting her, as she enters this strange, chaotic world.

Some merchants sell stacks and stacks of dried lizards, legs splayed out on wooden crosses, grisly crucifixes. Several stands display large shallow bowls or baskets filled with live scorpions, which crawl frenetically up the sides of the bowl only to slip back down again. Stacked coils of dried snakes are piled high on tables; exotic root vegetables and herbs that look like gnarled human limbs are arranged in baskets and crates.

The produce stands are riotous with color—yellow, orange, red, green; melons and fruits, bursting with life, paragons of freshness, more beautiful than any I've seen in my corner grocery store, or on the prosperous streets of Paris. No shrink-wrap, no

plastic, just the beauty of the fruits displayed in tiered arrange-
ments of rustic wooden crates. I want to reach out, and so I do; I
take a large fuzzy peach into the palm of my hand, and let it rest
there, feeling its weight. A man behind the counter puts up two
fingers, and I hand him some coins. When I bite into the fruit, a
savory burst of flavor fills my mouth and I smile at him, and the
old farmer returns my smile.

I move on, coming next to a stand that is dedicated solely to
the subtleties of rice. Thirty or forty bags of rice, each with a
slight variation in price written on signs planted among the
grains. I cannot read the signs, as they are printed only in Chinese, but they no doubt tell of what distinguishes one bag of
white grains from another almost identical one. I reach into
one bag and pinch a few grains between my fingers, and bring
them to my nose. A nutty, pleasant aroma wafts to my nostrils. I
do the same with grains from the next bag, and yes, they do
smell different, and I see now that one grain is slightly longer
than the other.

In America, rice is rice. It's white, it sits on the plate next to
the broiled chicken or fish, and it usually comes from a box. In
China, it is a staple, but much more than that. Rice feeds this
nation; it is the backbone of the society, served at every meal in
every household for thousands of years. It is displayed with the
respect it deserves, and shopped for carefully, like the fruit, like
the vegetables.

There are live creatures here too; dogs, cats, floppy-eared
rabbits, all waiting in cages to be bought, killed, and skinned on
the spot. Maggie stops and stares at two skinned rabbits lying
on the counter. She looks at the cages filled with live bunnies in
line behind them, and she seems to be processing this, brows
knit together, putting two and two together. I wonder if the

world will be different for her now, now that she knows there are places where they skin and eat bunnies, and kitties, and puppies; but after a few moments she shrugs her shoulders and skips off to the next curiosity, acceptance granted.

There is nothing hidden here, no falseness. I think of the grocery store back home, everything shrink-wrapped in plastic, a sell-by date stamped on each package. One advantage of seeing your dinner killed in front of you is that you never need wonder at its freshness.

We stroll for a long time, and I repeatedly glance back, keeping a watchful eye on Baby. As we wind through the streets of the market I start to feel comfortable, the strangeness wears off. Perhaps not all modernization is improvement after all. I like the human-scale living of this place, the way people shop for just enough food to fulfill that day's needs. I envision myself here, in this life, basket crooked over one arm, picking melons, a small bag of rice, or even a dried lizard or two. Yes, yes, I think; it is not at all impossible to imagine.

We reach the stairs to the overpass that brought us here, and Anna is standing just ahead, waving us on, guiding us once again into the modern world. Just before I reach her, I see a woman crouched down beside a tattered nylon suitcase. In the suitcase is something I cannot identify—it looks like bones, there is something sticking out. . . . I move forward, and crouch down beside her. She is a young woman, and there is a baby sleeping on her back, swaddled in a dirty cloth papoose. The woman wears a chunky stone ring on her left hand, and a large medallion swings from a cord around her neck. She looks up at me with a tired tolerance that seems to ask, "What do you want?"

I look down at the suitcase, and keep looking until my brain can put the pieces of this puzzle together. Yes, they are bones, large femurlike bones, with huge curved black claws attached to them by a tangle of gristle. Bear claws. Beside the bear claws in the suitcase are also horns of different lengths and colors, an exotic collection of hunter's trophies.

I am intrigued, and pull my camera from my backpack. I want to record this scene, but as soon as the woman sees the camera, she begins waving her hands in alarm and saying something that must mean "No, no!" She turns her head away, shielding her face from the offensive object. Just as she turns her head away, I see a small round button pinned to her shirt. It is a picture of a monk, with a shaved head and orange robe.

She must be a Buddhist—could she have come here all the way from Tibet? Perhaps this is an annual trip to the market, to sell the parts collected over the year. And now I have intruded upon her mission, disturbed her peace. I have heard that some people believe that when your photograph is taken, part of your soul is taken too. How many souls have I stolen? How many times has my own been divided?

I reach into the pocket of my jeans, and pull out some of my Chinese money, a few bills, and place them beside the torn and dirty suitcase that holds the woman's treasures. She does not turn to look at me, suspicious now, not willing to yield. I feel chastised, contrite; I want to apologize, but there is no way to say it. She is of her world, and I am of mine, and I leave her, in the China we have visited across the bridge of time.

∽

When we get back to the hotel, Alex takes Baby upstairs to put her down for a nap. I am glad to be alone, there is nothing to do but wander this giant place and nurse the feelings of sadness that have arisen again during the walk back from the market. This is how it has been for the past seven days: feeling sadness and fear, and then later a transition to acceptance and peace, with an eventual drift back into an even deeper despair that I then have to dig my way out of. I am exhausted by this effort to stay in balance, by the strain of trying to process so much emotional information. It may take the rest of my life to integrate all of this, if I ever do.

Ambiguity is one of the most difficult things to tolerate, and the intolerance leads to poor choices. Not knowing, not knowing how something will turn out, leads to impatience for an outcome. The impatience then results in one of two actions: either a resolution is forced, or there is a move to retreat, to give up. Either way, the result cannot be optimal, for in every situation, a process is working, an intricate, complex process, which has as its goal the highest outcome, the good of the whole, which we cannot easily see or grasp. This ability to allow the process to work can be called faith, and this faith is not a belief, this faith is not passive. The self-discipline needed to overcome the anxiety of ambiguity takes enormous effort to sustain.

The truth is that every single moment of every single life is uncertain. We go to great lengths to deny this, so much do we crave the illusion of security. It is as if the knowledge of this ambiguity is too terrible to bear, we must anesthetize ourselves in myriad ways or we won't be able to live the false lives we have constructed. True power lies in accepting the fact that everything is uncertain in every moment; it is the truth, and it is where our freedom lies. A small shift in thinking, a slight willingness to admit the possibility, and one can see that if everything is uncertain, then anything is possible.

Anything is possible. I could get Baby, even though in this

moment it looks doubtful. It is the certainty of those who are telling me it can't be done that appalls me. The only certainty is the love I feel for her, the only real and solid thing. Everything else is malleable, any regulation is subject to change, any man-made obstacle could crumble unexpectedly. Those who don't understand this fact are always surprised by the turn of events; but I intend to be ready and waiting to scoop up my treasure when all moves aside. The optimal outcome is the only one I will accept.

My only hope is to embrace the uncertainty, rejoice in the ambiguity, let the process proceed. The back-and-forth-ness of this situation has produced a sort of numbness, a state of sus-pended animation, which gives me the feeling that I am a wit-ness to myself, as if a part of me were watching from outside. I see myself walking, talking, acting, and feeling, and yet there is also a silent part watching, like a stereotypical Freudian thera-pist, nodding its head, saying, "Very interesting!" but maintain-ing emotional detachment. I am so grateful for it; the witness allows a buffer between me and the overwhelming emotions, the confusion and fear.

I think about Alex, about the true reasons behind her rejec-tion of Baby, things she has been saying these last few days to explain to me, to explain to herself, how this mess could have happened. It is true that she doesn't love her; but any love is blocked from coming forth by her inability to accept that which she did not expect. Baby is smaller than she thought she would be, she is younger, she was dirtier, she is needier. Baby doesn't look like she expected, her nose is too small. And most of all Alex doesn't feel the way she expected to feel, but those feelings were choked off by her own inflexibility. Things must be as she has decided to expect, or she rejects them, they are not real. Instead of deciding to work with and overcome her anxiety, she decides to reject the reality that has caused the anxiety.

If she had worked through it, if she had not let her fear win, what could the outcome have been? For Alex, a profound healing of her heart and a relief from her exhausting need for control; for Baby, a mother that could love her. But the intensity of Alex's fear, the almost total panic she experienced at the thought of raising this baby was too big an obstacle. The struggle between fear and reason has caused what I perceive to be almost a break in her psyche, something like a classic nervous breakdown.

But things are not as they appear, as Josephine has reminded me so many times. Beyond the psychological terminology is a deeper reality; it is as if a whole new side of Alex's personality has emerged, and is now living side by side with the old. It is almost as if two personalities reside there, and control keeps flipping back and forth between the two. In any given moment I do not know which side will emerge to be dealt with.

She is at war with herself, and all that has happened here is collateral damage. So I pray for her, that she finds a way to let love win.

❧

In the hotel lobby is a shop selling clothing and gifts, and as I stroll past I notice displayed in the window a pair of tiny Chinese cloth shoes. They are unusual, a blue and white brocade fabric accented with bright red piping. For some reason the sight of them stops me cold; I stand and look at them for a long time before I go inside and ask to see them. A young salesgirl reaches into the window and pulls them out, and places them in my upturned palm. They are as light as a feather, the soles are made of woven straw, they are beautifully made, they are perfect. I stand just looking at them, stroking them, turning them over in my hand, they feel just right.

Baby has been wearing shoes that Alex brought for her, the baby shoes that her son wore, many years ago. Alex has been concerned each day that they will get lost, she is always checking to make sure Baby has not kicked one off or that one is not untied. She wants to keep them for her son, a keepsake. They don't look right on Baby, they are scuffed boy shoes. They are not hers. I am sure that she has never had her own pair of shoes.

I tell the salesgirl that I will take them, and she carefully lifts them from my palm. She takes them behind the counter and tells me, "We will sew button on now." She takes a needle and thread from a sewing basket and begins attaching the little brown button that will fasten the strap across the instep of the tiny foot that will rest inside.

She takes such care as she pulls the thread in and out, making long movements with her arm, aiming for precise placement of the needle. She finishes quickly, and fastens the straps, and holds them up for my approval. Yes, they are perfect, I say, through the lump in my throat. The addition of the simple sturdy button makes them come alive somehow; they are infused with the loving touch of the salesgirl. She wraps each shoe carefully in a fresh piece of tissue paper and then wraps them both together into a tight bundle. She hands it to me, smiling and bowing her head slightly. I feel tears spring to my eyes; I take the bundle and thank her, but silently now because my voice will not come.

Outside the store I take the precious bundle and tuck it deep inside my backpack, on the very bottom, where no one will see it. This is my secret talisman, my act of faith, my leap into the arms of the possible. I have shoes for Baby, waiting for her little feet to fill them. They will be my symbol of hope, and a reminder that sometimes we must walk through pain to get home again.

இ

That evening, we go out into the streets of Guangzhou. The city comes alive at night, after the heat of the day subsides. People sit on stoops, and others stop to talk as they walk by. The shops are all open, and the proprietors stand at the entrances, trying to entice shoppers to enter. The air is warm and fragrant, and the waning light bathes the buildings in a golden glow, softening the edges. We walk the lovely streets near the hotel, and decide to eat dinner in a small restaurant called, mysteriously, The Cow and the Bridge.

Seated at a long table in the center of the restaurant, the group is lively and seems happy and relieved. After so many days of pressure, of worrying if something might go wrong along the way, there is elation that tomorrow we will fly to Hong Kong, we are free to go. Our new lives with the babies can begin, though my own and Baby's situation is far from certain. We still don't know if or how this adoption can be done, and from time to time a cloud of worry crosses my mind.

After dinner we stroll along the street. I notice a vendor selling jewelry, and realize that except for the baby shoes, I have not bought one souvenir from my trip to China. There are colorful bead bracelets and I select one and pay for it with the last of my Chinese bills. I lean down and show it to Baby in the stroller, she puts her fingers on it and then tries to put it into her mouth. I laugh as I slip it onto my wrist, thinking it has been anointed by her, I will always remember that.

I show Alex and she says, "I don't want anything to remind me of this trip. I hate China, I can't wait to get home." She is impatient now, and can hardly maintain the most basic social responses. When Louise asks her if she is anxious to get home so that her husband can meet the baby, she answers, "You have no idea!" and walks away, leaving a bewildered Louise on the sidewalk behind her.

Alex catches up to me and Baby.

"I talked to Louise last night," she says. "I went to her room while you were still out. I told her I was having problems . . . that I wasn't really bonding with the baby, and that I was upset that the agency lied to me about her age. She told me that things were a little rocky for them, too; not with their baby, but between her and Jimmy."

It occurs to me then that all of the adoptive parents in this group have seemed to be in some form of distress. Alex and her refusal of the baby is one example; Louise and Jimmy are another. Curtis and Judy are self-contained and have not confided any problems to the others, but in observing them, it is clear that this has been extremely stressful for them as well. When taken together, this could all just be evidence of the extremely intense nature of an international adoption; or it could be that none of these couples had adequate emotional preparation. From my conversations with Alex, I know that no preadoption counseling was provided by their agency.

"What did she say?" I ask. "Was she surprised?" When Alex shared with me the comment Jimmy had made, about my being Baby's mom, she told me she was going to try to assuage their suspicions by offering some information, without giving too much away.

"Not really; she said she had noticed we had been a little withdrawn from the group." That was an understatement; we had been purposely keeping to ourselves, trying not to let anyone know what was going on. I think ruefully of my early plans to talk extensively with the other parents, to find out about their lives, how they came to the decision to adopt from China.

"She was a little surprised when I told her I was upset that the baby was so young; their baby is even younger, only nine months old, and that's fine with them."

I don't understand Alex's obsession with the age of the baby either. From what I have been told by the other parents, designating the age of the child you are matched with has never been part of the deal. There is no way to know exactly what age these children are anyway, as they are all abandoned anonymously. The age is determined by an overworked orphanage director and is a guess at best.

We stop in front of a little convenience store and I ask Alex if she will wait with Baby while I go inside. I am looking for bottled water, but see a freezer filled with ice cream cups and decide to purchase one for Baby.

Back outside, I lean down in front of Baby in her stroller and open the cup of ice cream. I dip the plastic spoon into the hard surface and bring a scoop up to Baby's lips, thinking, She's going to love this. She sticks out her tongue and tentatively touches the foreign substance, and then immediately makes a grimacing face and spits the little bit of ice cream out onto her chin. It dribbles down and onto the front of her dress, and she puts her fingers into it and tries to wipe it away.

"Okay, Baby!" I laugh. "No more ice cream for now!" The sweetest things in life she will have to learn to love, in time. As we walk back to the hotel, I whisper to Baby of all the things I am going to show her and give her, and tell her that she deserves the best in life, that life has so much to offer.

"Ice cream is only the beginning, Baby, you'll see!" I say. With each passing moment, the dream of our future shines brighter and brighter, a brilliant star guiding me onward.

The midwife's name was Huong, and she explained to me the special preparations for bringing a lotus child into the world.

"There can be no doubt that this child will be endowed with a very high level of consciousness, even at birth. And we must ensure that as she passes from your body she is welcomed by those who know of her gifts. Those who do not know will be disturbed by the energy that she will embody, and may seek to harm or even destroy her. This is one reason why children are abandoned by parents. One or both parents are so disrupted by the energy—their own frequencies and the child's being so discordant—that the child is banished. This happens when the child is at a higher level of consciousness than the parents, and not the reverse; a rejected child is most usually one who will serve to challenge the parents beyond their capacity to grow spiritually," Huong explained.

I felt a wave of relief as I understood her words. "Then one with like frequency may love the child, may even be more compatible with the child than its own natural parent? And there could be one who could love my child, just as I myself would?" I asked.

Huong nodded vigorously. "Indeed, Empress! For the natural parent is a birth channel for the baby, but not necessarily the spiritual parent of the child. The spiritual parent of the child is one who has reached the same level of awareness, or higher. And so do not fear, for I know there will be one who will care for your child in just such a way, and guide her to attainment of all that is good, all that is of love."

The next morning, we gather our belongings and prepare to leave Guangzhou for Hong Kong, the last leg of our journey before we leave China. Moving about the room, packing my belongings, I think back to the dream of the night before, and wish I had the time to write it down in my journal. It seemed significant, it feels as if I learned something of importance in the night, and right now I can't quite grasp what it is. I would need time to think back, to focus on the dream images and bring them up from the depths. Perhaps later, when we arrive in Hong Kong, I'll be able to find time to be alone, and to think back over this and all the other dreams.

Later, standing in a long line in the heat of the airport terminal with mounds of luggage, baby strollers, bags, and boxes, the three families say good-bye to Anna. She shakes the hand of each of the parents, solemnly, bowing a little; she hugs and kisses each of the babies, and tells them good luck. When she holds Baby, Anna has tears in her eyes; they are just barely visible before she wipes them away with the back of her hand.

"Anna," I ask, "what do you think she'll be like when she grows up?"

She thinks for a moment, peering into Baby's face. "She will be pretty," she declares, "and . . . naughty!" She laughs with hearty delight at the thought of what "naughty Baby" will be like for her parents to raise.

"Naughty!" I exclaim. "Why naughty?"

"Well," she explains, "girls from each place have a reputation: girls from Canton sweet, girls from Shanghai smart, girls from Jiangxi have hot temper! But"—and she raises her forefinger, lest I think it's all bad news—"are hard workers!"

I laugh at her comments, thinking how perfect those traits are for living in America. I take her hand then. "Thank you, Anna, for all your help here in China," I say. "You've been a wonderful guide." I have come to like Anna very much, to appreciate her gentle demeanor, her efficient work habits, and her warm heart. It is clear that she cares about these babies, and is happy for them that they are going to have families, and that they are going to America. As far as I know, Anna has no idea that Baby's fate is uncertain, that Alex doesn't want to adopt her, or that she may be with me; I wonder what she would think. She hands me her business card and I glance down to see a Chinese name, her real name; she has finally revealed herself to me. I put the card carefully into my pocket, and make a vow that someday, I will contact her again, and tell her this story.

Anna kisses Baby on the cheek. "Good-bye!" she says to her, and hands her hastily to me and turns away, not wanting anyone to see the emotion she is trying to hide. She moves quickly away and does not look back, she is swallowed by the crowd; and then we are alone, and it feels strange.

Alex and I stand uncertainly with our belongings, passing the baby back and forth, playing with her, while the line moves slowly toward the checkpoint. Already the little group has started to disintegrate, each family moving away a little from the others, finally to have some space and distance. It is a relief. We are tired of pretending, tired of questions the others ask, tired of having to cover the truth of the situation. Every time someone has asked Alex about day care or preschool or what the baby's room is like, I have turned away. Every time someone has called the baby by the name Alex was to give her, I have cringed. It is excruciating because I am afraid it will make Alex change her mind and want to keep Baby. Each time the fear arises I must work it down, work it down, until I can move on and not be paralyzed by it.

Now that we are almost home—in only two days we will be landing in the United States—the anxiety should be lessening, but instead it is building inside me. Walking a tightrope for ten full days, my nerves are on edge, frayed and frazzled. And during these next two days, we have nothing to do; no adoption proceedings, no travel, no distractions. Just me, Alex, and the baby, and plenty of time to think.

And tomorrow is my birthday; I will be spending it in Hong Kong. My sister has arranged for Alex and me to stay at one of the nicest hotels in the city, the Four Seasons Regent, where she knows the manager and was able to get us reservations. I have been looking forward to this part of the trip particularly, have been planning on doing some Christmas shopping and having a nice meal to celebrate. Now it seems like just another day to get through, an unfortunate casualty of an unforeseen situation, and I am too tired to care.

Finally we board the flight, more than an hour later than scheduled. It is dark outside now, and as we rise above the tarmac, the lights of Guangzhou twinkle below. The lights spread out in a giant pool, as far as the eye can see.

Baby lies with her head upon my chest, not fussing or squirming, so adaptable, so accepting. What must these last days have been like for her? The first year of her life she was confined to a crib, or a chair; at most, the world consisted of the one room in the orphanage where she was placed. I doubt she went outside much, if at all; the visual and auditory stimulation now must be overwhelming. Colors, sounds, movement, music, languages, faces, tactile sensations, all encountered for the first time. A kaleidoscope of stimuli, a whirling puzzle of information. How is her little brain processing all of this, not to mention her emotions, fears, and hopes? I smooth her thin black hair, kiss her head; she grabs my index finger with her tiny hand and holds on.

My heart thumps against my chest, I love you, Baby! Just then, Alex looks over and sees the tender moment. She reaches out with her finger and strokes the baby's cheek, starts cooing at her to get her attention. The baby lifts her head, Alex reaches for her and lifts her from under the arms, away from me, and begins playing patty-cake, and Baby laughs, delighted. Alex puts her head next to Baby's, making kissing noises, talking in a singsong voice.

My stomach churns over, Oh, don't watch! Don't respond! I lean over and take a paperback from my bag, open it, and stare at the pages, reading one paragraph over and over, and not understanding any of it. The litany of comforting phrases I have been using to assuage my anxiety begins in my head: I do not own her, no one owns her; she belongs to herself, not to me, not to Alex. Feeling this love has to be enough, it doesn't have to turn out any one certain way, not the way you want it to. Only what is best for her, only what is best. Oh, God, I stand aside; only what is best.

I stand aside. I stand in faith that the best outcome will prevail, even if it doesn't look that way to me. And right now, it doesn't look that way to me. I feel myself slipping into that abyss of doubt; of course, what was I thinking, that it would work out? That I would bring this baby home? I have forgotten, so many times, the obstacles. And anyway, a voice says, this is all an exercise for you, a test for you. On the eve of your thirty-seventh birthday, have you learned anything? What have you learned? Will you live what you have learned?

The voice shocks me out of my cycle of repetitive thoughts: have I learned anything, will I live what I have learned? Yes, yes; that is the question, in any moment—each situation that arises is an opportunity to live what you have learned. If I let this opportunity pass, I will just have to live this point again, in another time, in another place. I may delay slaying these dragons on this battlefield, but I will meet them again on another, they will be the same dragons. I want to break through it now, while I have the chance, but how? How?

See the lesson, it is the only way. I see her face, she is happy, smiling, laughing. And I hear again the voice, and it tells me, her happiness is yours; all happiness is yours, if you choose it to be.

I reach down and put the book away. And I turn to face the scene that has aroused fear, envy, sadness, anger, all the things that cause pain and limit perception. As I face the scene that has given me a chance to move beyond these things, I say a silent prayer: Thy will be done.

の

The flight is mercifully short. Hong Kong airport is new and sleek and shiny, and we walk for miles in the immense open space, looking for baggage claim, trying to find customs. All the signs are in English, and it is easy to find our way, but our load of bags and gear is too much for one person to handle alone, as one of us must always be occupied with the baby. We have piled our stuff precariously on a large wheeled cart, and I push carefully; but still a piece slides off here, something gets caught in the wheel there, and we have to stop the whole parade, and reposition the stack.

I do this ten, maybe fifteen times, huffing and sweating, and cursing my tendency to overpack. This episode is perfectly sym-

bolic of the entire trip: there is too much baggage; something
falls off, I put it back; we move a few steps forward, and something else hits the ground and I have to stop again to retrieve it.
I am beginning to wonder if this trip will ever end.

And then, after what seems like a lifetime of this, a uniformed driver from the Four Seasons Hotel appears, and within
minutes he is loading our bags and us into a spacious black Mer-
cedes sedan that is polished to a mirror shine. The smell of the
leather permeates the car; there is enough room in the plush
backseat for both of us to lie down if we wanted to. I am stunned
by this feeling of luxury, such a contrast to the transportation we
have grown accustomed to these past days in China. It is heaven
on wheels.

Baby seems to like it too; she has perked up considerably
and is playing on the floor between the seats. I can't move,
weakened by our sudden catapult into yet another world, a
world of comfort and peace. Sealed inside the car, Alex and I do
not disturb the silence, do not intrude upon each other's
thoughts. I watch out the window on my side of the long backseat. I could ride like this forever, surrounded by the richness of
space and silence, a purgatory but at least a pleasant one.

But the ride does end, and in no time the car is zipping into a
circular drive in front of the glass doors of a tall modern building. The door is opened from the outside as soon as the car
comes to a halt. Another uniformed employee helps us out, then
scurries around to the trunk to retrieve the stroller, and helps us
load Baby into it. He ushers us inside, telling us the bags will be
brought up right away, to our rooms. "We have it all arranged
for you, no need to check in. We'll take you directly to your
room and make you as comfortable as possible," he says, and I

wonder if I am hearing correctly. We are being treated like royalty, or at least like some minor celebrity.

My sister must have asked her friend the manager to give us special consideration, and right now, I appreciate it so much I want to cry. Beauty, order, courtesy, softness, quiet; fresh flowers fill the lobby, soothing music wafts through the air. Plush rugs, gleaming marble, the hushed arrival of the elevator that will whisk us to our room. Low lighting in the hallway, nothing glaring or harsh. We enter our room and it is a lovely cocoon of comfort. The bellman goes to the window, and pulling the cord hand over hand, opens the curtain to reveal the most stunning view I have ever seen. The panorama of the Hong Kong skyline spools out before us, the colorful lights on each building celebrating the arrival of the new millennium, in just three weeks.

I stand transfixed at the window. I had almost forgotten. Christmas is fourteen days away, the New Year a week later. My birthday is tomorrow. For the first time since this trip began, I am oriented in time, in space. A huge Chinese dragon made of light spans the length of the skyscraper directly across the harbor from our window. The coming year will be the year of the dragon, a power year, a year when mighty and mythic forces are unleashed in the world. Anna told us that the dragon is symbolic of the spirit of the Chinese people, and that a dragon year is thought to be particularly lucky, a good year for beginning new undertakings.

Dragon, dragon, spirit of China, beautiful flaming beast; are you real, or imaginary? The Chinese call their land "Middle Kingdom," because legend has it that it floats between heaven and the underworld. Upon death the Emperor was believed to climb onto the back of the dragon and fly to his place in the heavenly realm. I am in my own Middle Kingdom, and I await my dragon, my flight to heaven, my own new beginning.

◆

My child never cried. For days following her birth I lay with her, she suckling at my breast, content and happy in the warmth of my arms. I sang to her, spoke to her, held her close; she was a world, and I entered that world completely, so that I hardly knew another world outside existed. Time stretched out, so that we lay together for an eternity, and all space contracted to the room in which we existed.

I was dimly aware of people coming and going. Shiu Lin, Huong, and even Chen moved about the room, bringing us food and water, but not disturbing our intense concentration, one upon the other. We looked into each other's eyes, and she spoke to me without words. She reminded me of a baby bird, and that is what I called her . . . Little Bird, my Little Bird. Though she had been given a name, I never used it; for to me, she was the essence of something so sacred that it must remain nameless.

I memorized her body, her face, her smell; I breathed her in like a fragrance, through every pore of my skin. I whispered to her that though in time we would be parted, nothing would stop me from finding her again, in this life, or in another, and I promised her that I would return again and again to the wheel of life, just to be reunited with her, and that my heart would recognize her, no matter what her form.

Shiu Lin began bringing me garments, and I would sew while the baby slept. The tray of imperial jewels lay upon the bed, and I would pick them, one by one; an emerald, a ruby, diamonds, pearls. I lay them inside an opened seam, and then sewed the pouch tightly shut, hiding my tiny stitches as best I could. Many garments I prepared in such a way, gowns and tunics, overshirts and underthings, so that my child would be telephone makes me jump, but Baby goes on sleeping, as does Alex, snuggled beneath a mound of covers on the other bed.

I reach the phone and pick up the receiver, say a quiet "Hello?" so as not to awaken them; my husband's voice comes over the line, and the first thing he says is, "Happy Birthday!"

I tell him I'm not sure how happy it will be; I am exhausted, and focused only on getting us home tomorrow. "Well," he says with a mischievous tone, "maybe this will help: we can adopt the baby, we have it all figured out!"

I sit in stunned silence, afraid to believe, how could it be that simple? Just two days ago he said that there was no way this could work. What has happened, how has he gone from "no way" to "it's done" in forty-eight hours? Here is the miracle I have been expecting.

"I called Josephine. . . ." he says. This is surprising. They have never spoken before. He knows very little of the conversations I've had with Josephine these past months. I keep our work together mostly to myself, for fear he might not understand. But somehow, he was moved to call her because, he says, "I did not know what else to do."

"What did she say?" I ask.

He tells me that she said that the important thing now, while the outcome was not yet clear, was for him to make a stand, to declare his intentions. "Do you want this child?" she kept asking him, over and over again, until all his qualified answers of "buts" and "ifs" were exhausted, and he finally said a clear and definitive "Yes." He tells me that when he said it, he felt a literal lifting of his spirit, as if something that had been weighing him down was now removed, and he was free.

He then called a friend, someone who had adopted two children and who knew of an agency that could help us; and after

arrayed in jewels of value beyond price, a treasure invisible
cannot see.

There is a legend in China of the mighty dragon tha
curely under its chin a bright pearl, the most fortunate o
this pearl that is the source of the dragon's power, for it mu
thing that it touches. If placed in a bag of coins, more coins
if settled into a sack of wheat, the wheat sack shall bulge v
crease wrought by the pearl.

I chose a large glowing pearl from the tray and held it b
fingers, caressing its smooth spherical surface. If I placed th
pearl, next to my baby's heart, perhaps more children such
would come, would grace earth with their presence. I placed
into a small cloth pouch and began to sew, each stitch b
hopes in place, my dreams for my baby, my dreams for my pe
a multitude of children spring forth, I prayed; may China b
their light. Oh, dragon of China, mythical beast of the land!
child, protect these children, for they have come to save the w

❧

Where is she?

I sit bolt upright, and throw the heavy covers back
am I? My heart is pounding; I cannot get a grasp of
roundings. An almost dark room, a curtained window,
crib . . . a crib. Yes, yes, the crib, for Baby. I take a deep
and remember, I am in Hong Kong, this is our last
China, we are going home. I throw my legs over the side
bed and walk to the crib, I need to see Baby and make s
is all right.

She sleeps peacefully on her back. I can hear the
breathing and I feel a sense of relief, from what, I do not kn
I am peering through the bars of the crib, the startling ring

speaking with a lawyer at the agency, it was clear that there was a process for this type of adoption, and the lawyer laid out the steps. I listen to the details, but keep thinking over and over, I knew this would be the outcome, I knew there was a way. How did I know? It's as if all along someone has been whispering in my ear that this is meant to be.

My husband tells me that the lawyer said that if, when we return to the United States, Alex still does not want to keep the baby, we should prepare to meet right away in his office so that Alex and her husband can sign papers that turn the baby over to the Virginia foster care system. The baby will then be placed with us as our foster child, and we will begin an immediate domestic adoption. That adoption will go through all the usual steps, including home studies and a legal hearing in six weeks. At that hearing, all legal ties between Alex and the baby will be severed, and it will be only a matter of a few months' wait for the domestic adoption to work through the system.

My husband is elated. He is giddy with happiness, and the last thing he says is, "Bring our daughter home."

I hang up and Alex pushes back the covers. "What's going on?" she asks in a sleepy voice. I tell her what he has said, how it can work, and she jumps from the bed and grabs me in a hug. "Oh, thank God! This is an answer to my prayers!" she says, and she is crying. It is genuine emotion, and I feel a strength and calmness spread over me, that no obstacle remains, and all will be well.

I tell Alex I want some time to myself; Baby is still sleeping, it is just barely dawn. I leave the room and find the rooftop terrace that juts out over Hong Kong harbor. The misty morning air creates an ethereal scene, it is as if the terrace is floating in the clouds.

I sit on a little wooden bench, and think, How will I explain all of this to others, and to myself? I think of a time two years ago when I was having dinner with an old friend from college. She brought up the fact that, though I had professed for years that I wanted children, I remained childless to that day, even after more than ten years of marriage. "What are your plans?" she asked. "I'm just so concerned! I think you would be a great mother, and you know, we don't have forever, time is moving on!"

I thoughtfully considered what she was saying, and then told her that I knew what she was saying was true, but I was just not worried about it, and I didn't know why. "If it's meant to be, it will happen," I said. And she reminded me that for something to happen, I would have to take action of some kind. I told her not to worry, that I knew it would work out. We dropped the subject then for the rest of the dinner, but later, after sharing a bottle of wine and lots more conversation, we stood waiting for the car outside the restaurant. Suddenly I turned to her and said, out of the blue, "I know I will have one child, it will be a girl, and I will have her when I'm thirty-seven years old!"

She looked at me blankly, stunned at my declaration. "Well!" she said, after she recovered. "That was definitive! Where did that come from?" I looked back at her, shocked myself at what I had just blurted out. "I have no idea!" I said. And I did not.

Now, two years later, it is the morning of my thirty-seventh birthday, and my husband has just told me that we will adopt a child. A strange, unexplainable coincidence, just one more in a long list in relation to this situation. I have no explanations. And for now that is just fine, none are necessary.

I sit for a while and watch the boats in the harbor. When I return home tomorrow, my life will have been completely altered; I will not be going back to the life I left. I will not even be the same person I was before, and that is an answer to a prayer. For what does not change must die, and I want to live.

⌇

The face of the Emperor's concubine was before me. I turned to see the familiar cold glare, which left no question as to her resentment of me and of my place as Empress. I noted her hard beauty that had in the end served to disappoint her; for she had thought it would buy her the Emperor's heart and the key to power over all others, over all women whom she saw as rivals.

When I saw her, I jumped to my feet with a strangled cry. Han froze with his arms held high above his head, our Little Bird suspended in air for a moment, until he slowly lowered her to his chest, and turned his back to the one who would be our undoing.

I could not move and stood rooted in place, as the concubine moved slowly toward me, arms crossed, a smirk of cruel delight upon her face.

"And so, Empress," she drawled, "what do we have here? A child? How delightful!" Her hard eyes glittered above the pallor of her cheeks, flushed now with crimson from the excitement of her discovery.

"It has been so long since I, or anyone else in the palace, has had occasion to see you, and perhaps this explains why!" The concubine swayed her hips a little as she walked, taking mincing steps to prolong her advance.

"I suppose with the Emperor away for so long that you must have become bored and needed some . . . entertainment." Ling Dao laughed a terrible cheerless laugh. "Well. It appears that you have found it! For there is nothing more entertaining than a child, and such a beautiful one at that!" And she moved closer so that I could see the sallow cast of her skin, and smell the sweet heavy perfume with which she had bathed herself.

I stepped forward then, recovering my abilities. I placed myself between this woman and Han, between her and my child. "There is nothing for you to see here," I said, barely keeping my voice controlled. "You must go now, these are my private chambers." My heart was beating wildly, though I mustered the strength to appear unfazed at her intrusion.

"Oh, but I should love to see her!" she exclaimed with feigned delight. "It is a girl child, is it not? My, my, and so it is; what a pity. A son, now that is something of which to be most proud! I myself should like to bear a son, for only that is important to the imperial lineage," she said, her voice dripping with condescension.

I thought of my beautiful girl child, of the countless women and girls of this land, who for centuries had been enslaved by this philosophy, the idea that male children were of greater value and must be coveted. This idea was the justification for murder, brutality, and cruelty perpetrated by men and women alike, in homage to a freakish concept that had been allowed by all to become ingrained and unassailable in this society. I heard the concubine's words and understood her implication—she would betray her own kind for personal gain, and I feared for my people, feared for the soul of this land.

When I return to the hotel room, we dress, and go downstairs to the restaurant for breakfast. Baby sits in a high chair at the end of the table, gobbling up the scrambled eggs and bacon I have ordered for her breakfast. She seems stronger with each passing day; it is incredible to see how quickly she has responded to my care. Alex and I sit across the table from each other, and I exclaim several times about the view of the harbor from the restaurant windows. The floor-to-ceiling glass gives the feel that we are floating on the water, and the boats going by just outside seem close enough to touch. Alex nods or murmurs acknowledgment of my comments, but doesn't look at the view, or offer any thoughts of her own.

Alex sips her coffee. Then she looks at me and says, "Maybe we could be co-mothers."

I continue feeding Baby, thinking, Maybe if I pretend I did not hear . . .

But she goes on. "I could be part of her life. I could take her sometimes, when you go out of town. I could come to her ballet recitals . . . you know, be involved. What do you think? We could do this together."

I take a deep breath, put down my fork. If I speak, will I betray myself, will I betray the anger that has suddenly flared within? All this time, I have been struggling to keep my feelings under control; fighting to not think about how often Alex has been insensitive, thoughtless, or downright cruel. But this suggestion, that we be "co-mothers," pushes me toward the edge. I have to wait a few moments before I respond.

"I don't know how that would work, Alex; to be 'co-mothers,'" I begin. What is she saying exactly, that we would share this child? "I don't see anything wrong with you being involved somehow, but I don't think we should do anything that would be confusing to the baby. It's going to be tough enough to explain all this to her someday, the way it is, don't you think?" I say.

It is hard to maintain my composure; a volatile mixture of anger, fear, and confusion begins swirling inside me. Is she saying she has doubts again, that she really wants to be this baby's mother?

Alex calmly takes a sip from her coffee cup, and we fall into silence.

〜

We go out into the city. There is a place called Stanley Market where there are good things to buy, children's clothing and linens, souvenirs, silk robes, everything made in China, and sold for a pittance. We hail a cab in front of the hotel, and begin the long ride, through the city and along the curving highway that hugs the harbor. The view is breathtaking, the high hills surrounding the water, the buildings built precariously into their sides. I watch out the window, noticing how different Hong Kong is from mainland China. It is the West, the British influence is so obvious; and yet, the faces are Chinese. It is the nexus of two worlds.

I should be elated. This is my birthday; I have just found out that we can adopt Baby. I am in an exciting city and we are to spend the day exploring. And yet, an anxious nausea set in when I returned to the hotel room this morning, and has been increasing during the ride. There was something in my dream last night about relinquishing a child, my child . . . it was so disturbing and I try desperately to pick up the pieces of the broken memory. A basket . . . a baby . . . someone taking her away, the feeling of intense despair . . . and then it comes, before my mind:

> Chen entered from the garden carrying a basket over his arm. He placed it on the floor in front of me, and removed the lid. Tears glistened in his eyes as he showed me how to place her inside, snuggling her down so that she completely filled the cavity. This was how she had filled my body also, when I had carried her those months. Fitting so perfectly, the space meant just for her. I would never be filled like that again; this I knew. The empty place inside me gnawed like a hunger and I placed my

hand upon my belly as I leaned down to kiss the soft cheek and to say good-bye. Good-bye, Little Bird, good-bye. . . . In the last glimpse of my child, I saw silky lashes resting on creamy skin, the perfect rosebud lips, the sparse hair, and even as Chen placed the lid securely on the basket, I saw her there, sleeping in perfect trust. Something heaved in me as I thought, That trust will be broken; now it will be broken, and she will always be afraid.

Chen was to smuggle my child out of the palace by way of a path laid out by Han, to a place unknown to me. I was not to be told of her destination, to protect me from myself. Chen lifted the basket and carried the precious bundle away, not looking back as he rounded the doorway into the garden. The sudden emptiness of the room was impossible to bear. Their departure created a vacuum that collapsed around me, and I imploded in on myself. I fell to the ground under the pressure, not able to resist the power of my grief. I asked my God, How shall I live? Through this night, how shall I live, without my daughter, without my love? A night without dreams of a life, without any tomorrows?

And he answered me later, when the darkness had almost engulfed me; he answered me only when I could ask no longer. His answer was something I already knew, that the love was inside me and could never be lost.

Finally Chen returned from his sacred mission. The sight of me must have unnerved him, for he did not speak when first he saw me, but came into my chambers and sat upon the bed, put his head into his hands, and remained unmoving there.

I went to the cage that stood in the corner of my room, the cage that held the bird that Chen had given me those many mornings ago, on the day before I wed. I put my arm inside the opening, and the bird jumped upon it. Drawing it out, I turned to Chen, and held the bird out toward him. He shook his head. "I will not take it," he said. "I will not leave you."

I did not move, but continued to hold out my arm until finally he, too, brought up his arm, slowly, until the tips of our fingers touched, and as they did so we looked into the depths of each other's eyes. I saw in Chen's eyes the perfect love for me with which he made his choice. This is what saved him, transformed him, and made him whole, and this is what will draw us together, again and again, as we cycle through the earthly existence on the path toward perfection.

"All will be well," Chen whispered urgently as he gripped my hands in his. Just as I whispered, I have loved you so, the bird took flight across the slight gap between us, and landed safely on his outstretched finger. In the end, we must let go of everything.

The feeling of loss from the dream memory is unfathomable. How is it that we can experience emotions of such depth and complexity during a state of consciousness that is not considered "real," over events that have not even "really" happened? The body itself makes no distinction between dream and reality . . . during a dream of loss or fear, the corresponding chemicals are pumped into our bloodstream in exactly the same dose that would be pumped if the event had happened while awake. What, then, is real? The body certainly doesn't know, and mine is still feeling the effects of the dream emotions of last night.

And on top of this, once again, Alex's behavior has changed markedly. She is now so interested in Baby, wants to hold her and care for her—she got her dressed for our outing, and even now is playing patty-cake with her as she sits on her lap in the car.

I pretend as if I don't notice, I play along. But by the time we reach Stanley Market, I feel as if I'm going to cry. Not only is Alex displaying such maternal behavior, but Baby has begun to clearly favor her over me. When I try to hold her, she reaches for Alex, squirming to get back into her arms.

I try to reason myself out of despair. For one thing, I pulled away from Baby, just when she had bonded with me and felt secure. She had trusted me, and then I distanced myself. And though I knew the reasons for my actions, she could not; how could she understand what I had to do? I don't blame her, don't blame her at all. She is looking for what she needs, her survival is at stake.

But what of Alex's actions? What to make of them? I keep thinking, She has to know how this makes me feel, she has to know. Only a dunce would not see that this sort of back-and-forth would play havoc with my emotions, and she is anything but stupid. But this morning she seemed so sincerely happy that we could adopt the baby; is this now just innocent affection? Relief that now Baby will have a good home? But her behavior makes me feel so uncertain, what if she decides, after all this, that she wants her?

I don't want to ask Alex about her intentions, to even introduce the possibility into our conversation. And though I keep repeating the thought that she is mine, it does not matter what I tell myself; I feel sicker and sicker as we stroll through the market, my energy draining from me as the moments pass. I have to get out of here, I just want to go home; and by the time we finally hail a cab to return to the hotel, I feel it is the worst birthday I have ever had. All during the ride, Alex's heretofore unexpressed affection for Baby is in full bloom. She laughs with her, tickles her, plays fun games; and I think, I just can't do it, can't pull myself out of this one. I will just stay here in de-spair—you won, you won!

I do not know what to make of this. Of course I have to re-member that until there is a court hearing that severs her rights to Baby, Alex could change her mind at any time, and take Baby back. She would have every right; there would be nothing I could do to prevent it. Am I willing to live with that possibility? It could be months of such worry, can I handle it?

Outside the taxi window, the chaos of Hong Kong swirls in dizzying confusion, and for a moment my mind, exhausted and overwhelmed, slips into a groove that has been worn by the dreams of these past days, and I see the face from my nightmare of last night, the beautiful hard face of the concubine. It is there before me, so vivid for one moment that I am frightened and unsure if I am dreaming or awake. And then the image is gone, but a shiver runs through me and on a warm day in a tropical city my body goes cold as ice.

And then I look into Baby's laughing face, and decide not to let our future slip away.

そう

When we let ourselves into our hotel room, the phone is ringing, and I run to catch it. It is Josephine. While Alex gets Baby settled, I go into the other room so I can speak to her in private. "How did you know to call, on the worst day of my life?" I ask her.

"Worst day of your life? It's your birthday!" she exclaims. I tell her of today's events, how the morning started with such bright promise, and how the day has degenerated into a tangle of fear and doubts. A thicket of despair, I can't find my way out. . . . I tell her I have a bad feeling and I just want it all to be over. I want it all to be over, the pain, the ups and downs, the anxiety, and even the hope; the higher my hopes reach, the deeper my despair later; the higher the cost. "We anesthetize ourselves, don't we?" I say to her. I realize that I always have; that I've always chosen to do without heart-stopping joy if I could avoid the other end, the blind despair that comes with the inevitable loss of that joy.

Josephine tells me I need to find some time to be alone, to pray. "Have you been praying?" she asks. "Nonstop," I answer. "It just comes spontaneously now, I am always praying, always praying." I, who until now have had a hard time even saying the word God, who until now have only prayed the stale memorized scripts of the Catholic Mass. I am praying for my very life. I never understood about prayer, what it is, or what it is supposed to do, so I rejected it, never practiced it at all, until Josephine taught me that prayer is using your will to align the mind with the highest principles, to open a channel through which peace can come.

And then I tell her about the dreams, how this morning I woke up in a panic from a dream I can only half remember. The dream still won't let me go, snatches of it have been coming to me all day. It was a dream of loss, of endings and searching for salvation. The emotional tone has woven itself into my waking life so that I don't know if my sadness and loss of heart is its residual, or is caused by events of the day.

We talk for a long time, she giving me encouragement and me wanting to believe. She tells me that I must write down the dreams, that I must discover what they mean, that freedom lies in understanding.

"And one last thing," she says, before we hang up. "When you are on the plane tomorrow, when you leave China, hold the baby against your heart." I don't ask why, knowing that everything Josephine says has meaning beyond the obvious. She can see things that others can't; though she has told me over and over that she is not psychic. Her gift allows a glimpse into the world beyond this one, where our actions have consequences beyond our understanding.

So I just tell her that I will; it sounds so beautiful that I don't need reasons. In the other room, Baby is asleep. I tell Alex I'm going out for a while. I take the elevator once again to the rooftop terrace, and find it deserted and quiet and eerily still.

~

I sit on a bench overlooking the steely waters of the harbor below. I have often wondered, would it be possible for me to love an adopted child as much as one to whom I gave birth? Wouldn't there be a difference in intensity, or less of an identification, less of a bond? But what I know now is that love is a mysterious force, powerful beyond all measure. That I could love, so intensely, a child that some other woman had given birth to, defied my own conceptions of what love was. "Your children are not your children. They are the sons and daughters of Life's longing for itself," says Kahlil Gibran in *The Prophet,* and I know now that longing is the force that draws all living things together.

After a time of reflection, I take out my notebook. I feel something rise in me; an agitation, a release from lethargy. Joy unmasks itself in my heart.

> *For when fear and desire die, only the unspeakable reality of love remains.*

The memory of these words is a catalyst, my mind starts to reel back, to the first dream about China so many months ago. The voice of the woman, longing for her child, that came a year ago on the last night in the little white house . . .

And then it is like watching a movie unfold in my mind; I write as fast as I can, to keep up with the images. I write for a long time, until I realize I can barely see, it is now so dark. I move from the terrace into the hotel hallway, where there is a bench, and I continue writing, continue recording my dream of a life.

I write while tears stream down my face, tears of realization, tears of discovery. I begin to see, I see . . . all my life operating as if that were all there was of it; as if it had a discrete beginning and end, as if my choices in this life were determined only by the events of this life, when in reality this life is an echo of something begun long ago.

Those I have loved and needed and lost, cycling with me in desire to meet again, to try again to perfect our experience in this earthly domain. Friends, family, lovers, and enemies, all playing their parts through time, all seeking to balance the scales so that they may go home again.

Hours later when the pages are no longer empty and my tears have faded in the joy of knowing of a greater existence, I return to the room and begin to pack. We are going home, and all will be well.

∽

In the soft pink light of morning, I take Baby out in her stroller for one last glimpse of the land of her birth before we leave. Just as there was for me coming here, there will be repercussions for her as she enters a new country, a different world. She will have to get used to the sights, the smells, the sounds of a new language. In just a few hours we will get on a plane and fly home to those things, and to the possibility that we may not be together; but for now, I imagine that I can stop time, and hold her forever.

It is early morning and China is stirring; there are so many people out on the streets, so much life, this city is bursting at the seams. We walk the crowded sidewalks. People pass by but we interact with no one. For a time we sit, Baby in my lap, on one of the benches that line the promenade beside Hong Kong harbor and watch the cargo boats move slowly back and forth. Where are all these boats going filled with goods, filled to the brim with toys and clothes and things no one really needs, and meanwhile the things that everyone needs are in such short supply, like love, for instance, like compassion.

Perhaps I will never hold you again Baby, I think. Perhaps the things of the world, the rules and regulations of the world, will come between us. I don't know what will happen when we leave here. Was this all a dream too, something from which I'll awake to find I have lost you once again? I will try not to think of the possibility of separation now, with the reality of you pressed against me like this, so warm, so completely tangible. I will try to memorize the feel of you, in case this chance never comes again.

How is it possible to be reborn if you do not die?

If we are not together, I will long for you, always long for you.

It is my most urgent wish to be reborn. It is the only wish I have now, the only desire left to me. Everything else, all passion, all hope, slowly fades to the point where I cannot see it anymore. It is difficult for me to even imagine a time when passion moved me, or hope lifted me. I want nothing that I used to want, which makes me not the person that I used to be. We cre-

ate ourselves through what we desire, and I don't know who I
am anymore.

I want nothing of this world, nothing but to love you. What was false in me has died, and someday, I hope to speak to you of how these words came to me one night, when all seemed lost. These words came to me as a gift, as a miracle, just as you have come.

What you have given me is beyond value, beyond price; what can I give you in return? It is my greatest wish that you be whole, and happy and free. I have never wanted anything so much, yet felt at such a loss to achieve it. You represent all that is good in the world, in triumph over all that is bad.

Gently I pull you from where you are huddled against my chest and you reluctantly allow this separation. The wind ruffles your hair, your infinite eyes gleam, and in them I see the only thing of any real value in this world, the spark of a human soul. Your arms reach out, you want me to pull you close again, and I will; but first I want to give you what is rightfully yours.

You have been Baby, the nameless child. You have been the child with no home. You have been the forgotten child, deemed unworthy of identity. From now on, you will be who you were meant to be. Your eyes search mine, wondering at my intensity. I have seen you blossom like a flower in the sun; I have watched the flame of hope deep within you reignite amidst the embers of despair.

"Lily," I whisper. "Lily."

I know I have loved you forever.

୭

After Lily and I return from our walk through the streets around the hotel, my unnatural buoyancy seems to unnerve

Alex. She is quiet, withdrawn, while I happily get us all moved about, from the hotel to the airport, to our gate, onto the plane. We are settling in, the airplane is packed, a popular Hong Kong to San Francisco flight, filled to capacity.

I am standing with Lily, arranging our things, when a middle-aged woman approaches, looking quizzically at me and up toward the seat number.

"Nine-D?" she asks. "Are you in nine-D?"

"Yes," I tell her, "this is my seat."

"I have the same one, look!" and she hands me her ticket stub, and it says 9-D. I pull out my own; it too says 9-D; we have both been assigned the same seat. Irritation arises; can't this last part of the trip go smoothly? But the woman moves away, she goes to find a flight attendant who might solve the problem, and I settle into my seat, thinking, Squatter's rights; they won't make me move.

In moments the woman is back, flight attendant in tow. It turns out that the seat next to me is empty, the only one available on the flight. It seems we are destined to sit together, this woman and I, and she settles her belongings and immediately reclines in the seat, closes her eyes, and goes to sleep.

How can someone sleep when there is so much commotion going on, people boarding the plane, stuffing packages overhead and bags under the seat, flight crews making announcements over the intercom? But she is; my neighbor is snoring soundly. I look at her. She is around middle age, slightly overweight, a little disheveled. She is an Asian woman, but she spoke perfect unaccented English.

The plane finally taxis for takeoff, and Alex, sitting on my other side, also snuggles down to sleep. I hold Lily, and as the plane races down the tarmac, gathering speed for our ascent, I pull her to me, pull her to my heart. I feel hers beating next to mine, in perfect rhythm, and when at last we leave China, she looks up at me, and smiles.

༄

The dinner cart has reached us, and my neighbor finally stirs. She has been asleep since we boarded, and so has Alex. Lily fell asleep shortly after takeoff, and I was left to stare into space, keeping vigil; I have slept enough. I have slept a lifetime, and from now on sleep will serve only to awaken me.

We start to make conversation, the woman and I. Almost immediately she asks me about Lily. "Have you adopted her?" "Where is she from?" "What was the process like?" She is very interested.

I tell her my friend Alex has adopted her, I stick to the story. We have just left China, nothing is certain. The woman listens well; she nods and absorbs the story. I begin to see that she is a kindly and thoughtful person, that she asks good questions and makes astute comments. I tell her about visiting the orphanage, about the terrible problem of abandoned babies, mostly girl babies, and of my grief at having seen those who must be left behind.

"I left China long ago, when I was just a child," she tells me. "I have heard of this but have never traveled there to see." She tells me that she has lived in California for over twenty years now, and is an American citizen. I see a sadness when she speaks of China, and she gently steers the subject away, toward the life she has now, the one she has built in America.

"I am coming from India. I have spent two months there studying with a guru," she tells me. A Buddhist, she has devoted most of her adult life to studying and teaching. It is then I notice her jewelry, prayer beads around her neck, a medallion with a picture of a monk, a bead bracelet used for meditation. I ask her many questions about her practice, about going to India. And after a time she points to my wrist and asks, "And are you a Buddhist?" I am wearing the bracelet purchased from the street vendor in Guangzhou, the day we went to the market. It is a string of jade beads, very simple; it looks almost exactly like the one the woman has on her own wrist.

I almost forgot that I have it on. I take it between my fingers, seeing it, really seeing it, for the first time. Am I a Buddhist? How to answer this question? I do not practice any religion, but believe in universal truths. I am a Buddhist in that I believe that the Buddha spoke truth. But I am a Christian, too; I was raised Catholic and I believe that Jesus attained the ultimate in human potential, Christ consciousness, and that to follow his teachings, his authentic teachings, will save us.

"I am not a practicing Buddhist," I answer. "But I have studied the teachings, and accept them as truth."

The woman nods, and begins telling me that she recently saw the Dalai Lama, that she heard him speak at a conference, a gathering of Buddhists at a small college town in the Midwest.

A small college town in the Midwest . . . my mind slowly reels back, to a day just three months before, when I was running through the streets of my alma mater, having just arrived in town to deposit my stepdaughter at college. I saw a poster, in the window of the hotel lobby; apparently, there was a major event taking place there, just that weekend: the Dalai Lama, the spiritual leader, was to address an audience of thousands of Buddhists, and perform a rare ceremony that had something to do with enlightenment. He was there in this little town because his brother was administrator of a large Buddhist center there, and had invited him to come.

When I saw the poster I was overwhelmed with a desire to go, to find the gathering, to see the Dalai Lama. But we were to be in town only a few hours, we had to get back home. How could this be, to be in the same place at the same time as the eminent figure of the Dalai Lama? It was strange to think that our paths had come so close to intersecting, and in such an unlikely place.

I did not get to see the Dalai Lama. But now this woman, a native of China, a traveler from India by way of Hong Kong, a resident of San Francisco, who by some fluke happened to be assigned my seat on the flight, was telling me that she was there too. Our paths had crossed twice, in three months' time.

The shocked look on my face makes her ask, "What's wrong?" And when I tell her, "I was there too; I was in the same little town that same weekend that the Dalai Lama was there," she laughs a delightful tinkling laugh, and she almost seems like she is not surprised.

And suddenly, we both know that our meeting is no accident, no accident at all, and we begin urgently talking, putting our heads near each other's to catch every word. Just then, Alex gets up and leaves her seat, and I say to her, "I have something to tell you!" And I tell her the story.

৵৵

Her name is Grace. She tells me this as she pulls the jade amulet from the bag under her seat. Grace, yes . . . this has been a Grace, to have this woman next to me during this long flight to a new life. I unburden myself, for the first time since the ordeal began; I tell her of my hopes and fears and of the tremendous love that has blossomed in my heart. I tell her that something else is going on too, that there are dreams, that I suspect there was a past life connection between me and Lily. She listens with deep understanding, she nods and affirms.

She asks softly, "And why do you think your friend could not take her?" I tell her that I think, deep down, she was frightened of Lily . . . frightened of what it would take from within herself to raise this particular child. "She couldn't do it," I say, and she asks, "Can you?" And I get the feeling that her question is more than casual interest, as if she is a proxy and is receiving my answer on behalf of something much larger than herself. Her eyes hold intense expectation, and bore into mine. After a moment of reflection I answer, with no hesitation or restraint, "Yes," just simply, yes. And she smiles in relief and says, "That's right!" and begins to take things from her bag, as if by my answer she is free to bestow gifts upon Lily, in celebration of this event.

Grace brings forth a string of prayer beads, and says they were blessed by the Dalai Lama. "Hold these for her, so that she may use them later," she says, and I take them in my palm with reverence. Lily touches them; she is very gentle and acts as if she knows that they are holy.

Next she pulls out a medallion, which dangles from a thin red cord. On the medallion is a tiny painting of the goddess Kwan Yin on one side, and a photograph of a monk on the other. "See what she does when she sees this," she says, and holds it in front of Lily. Lily reaches for it, and looks for a long time. She flips it over and looks at the monk, and looks up at Grace; she looks down again. I look over to see Grace nodding, obviously pleased, but she does not tell me the significance of the medallion, or who is pictured on it. "Keep that for her," she says, and I put it carefully away with the prayer beads.

And then she takes the bracelet of beads from her wrist, the one that looks so similar to my own, and places it in my palm. "This is for you, from me," she says, and there are tears in her eyes as she holds my hand there. "You have both been blessed."

I feel a chill run the length of my body as she says these words, and I cannot speak. Alex returns to her seat and we spend the remainder of the flight in silence. Picking up the threads from a dream of last night, a dream of final clarity: palace guards . . . the Emperor's cruel face . . . his bed chamber, I can see it all in such perfect detail in my mind's eye. As the Emperor stood before me, his face took on many masks, one after the other, as he struggled with the terrible conflict that raged inside him:

The Emperor strode forward and fixed me with a purposeful glare. In his hand he held a pouch that bulged at the sides, and when he reached the bed, he held the pouch upside down above it. He loosened the cords and out tumbled all manner of jewels, and folded pieces of paper, which scattered about. I recognized the jewels. They were the ones I had sent out to help those in need, when Chen and I released our birds. So they had helped no one, for here they were.

I did not look at him, but kept my eyes upon the jewels. They were so beautiful and I wanted to pick them up and hold them to the light, to feel their weight and look into their depths. When the Emperor finally spoke it was with a cold, low voice. "You have betrayed me," he said. "You have betrayed the empire." I had known he would say these words, for the small mind of such a man can find in all events only reference to himself. A narcissistic will betrays all.

The Emperor pushed me backward onto the bed, and I did

not resist, for I knew it was futile. I lay down amidst the jewels
scattered there, while the Emperor strode back and forth, mut-
tering to himself in words I could not hear. An epic internal
struggle, the nexus of all choice, was upon him. Ego or spirit?
Love or fear? Humanity or brutality? Hope or despair? Life or
death? In every life there comes a time when the final choice be-
tween opposites must be made.

That time was upon him, and I watched as he struggled.
There was nothing I could do, as this choice represented the ul-
timate use of free will. This is the choice we all must make, all
and everyone.

After what seemed like an eternity in the dream, I saw his face
go slack, he had made his decision. There was something terrible . . . a snake, a writhing, angry beast, and the Emperor held it
by the jaws. I knew what would happen, the way you do in
dreams, but could not stop it. Pain, and a feeling of warmth
spread throughout my body, paralyzing my will little by little,
until there was the sublime feeling of dissolving into light . . .
and that was the last image from the dream: pure, white, all-
encompassing light:

The room swirled about me in a kaleidoscope of images,
faces of those I loved, scenes of beauty and tranquility, the re-
flecting pool with its lotus that serenely floated upon its surface.
When now it was certain I would begin my journey to another
time and place, I turned my thoughts to that which is eternal,
and what I saw was beyond any dream of heaven.

I felt myself evaporating into nothingness, losing that
thread that keeps us rooted upon the earth. And just before the
darkness fell, I saw a light so bright that I was blinded with the

brilliance, and felt a joy of letting go as I went to it, to the place
where all is one.

Strangely, I am not less myself, but more . . . for a death is nothing like what we suppose. Holding Lily, I know that all love is
returned to us in time. Sometime later, when the plane lands
and we rise to gather our belongings, I bend to pick up Lily, and
when I turn back to speak to Grace, she is gone.

~

At the end of the ramp I stop to put Lily into her stroller. "You
push her when we go out," Alex says to me, her voice tired and
strained. I am relieved, as I have been wondering, worrying
about this moment. Would Alex want to be in charge of Lily
upon our arrival, would it be an awkward moment? Both of
our husbands were to be there waiting at the gate, and I wanted,
so badly, to have her in my arms when my husband first saw
Lily. But Alex seems in a hurry to move ahead, and she walks
quickly away, not stopping to help get Lily situated in the
stroller.

I push her slowly up the ramp, my legs weak and shaky. I
can't walk faster, it is as if I am in the slow-motion world of a
dream. I look down at the top of Lily's head, she is sitting forward a little, expectantly.

Alex walks far ahead of us, she cannot get away fast enough.
I see her husband up ahead, she stops and he greets her; briefly
he looks up and catches my eye, and then they turn and he puts
his arm around her. She buries her head in his shoulder and
they walk away toward a life they were not expecting.

I don't have a chance to take the baby from the stroller before I see my husband. He is standing just inside the doorway,

at the back of a crowd of people knotted at the end of the ramp. He is standing on tiptoe, straining to look for us over the tops of the heads in front of him. His face holds a look of anxious expectation and hope; of joy denied, of dreams about to come true. Our eyes do not meet, he is looking for her, his daughter. And when he sees her, his face crumples in such a way that I know we have achieved an incredible victory of the heart, it is a divine reunion.

We reach him and he hugs me tightly to him. He stoops down and says hello to our baby. I kneel down too and everything in the world disappears, everything but the three of us.

We are laughing and crying; the pain of years, of lifetimes, burns away, leaving only our joy. There has been no time since we were last together, for time does not exist, and we go out into the world to begin again where once we left off, redeemed in love, our spirits whole, our souls renewed, this journey complete.

Epilogue

How do we know where our journeys may ultimately take us? Five years ago, I went on a trip, and returned with an understanding that life is not as we suppose. I returned with a baby, with a piece of myself, with the ability to see a pattern in what before had looked like chaos. Our lives, part of a tapestry, woven through time by threads of our choosing.

They say much has changed in China, in the five years since I found you here. But one thing I know has not: there are still countless baby girls who will never have the chance to experience life, who will never have the chance to walk these streets, inhale these smells, hope for the future, or bring joy into the world.

You hold my hand tightly as we weave through the crowded sidewalks, people jostling and staring, the sounds and smells of Hong Kong vibrating in the air around us. The expression on your face is serene and you hold your head high, not making eye contact with the many who try to do so. You are nearly six years old; where have you come by such dignity? Your very presence frees them of their guilt, Lily; perhaps you understand this.

Before, when we walked these same sidewalks, my deep agitation over what would become of us permeated my experience,
and everything I saw, smelled, and heard seemed foreign, sinister, threatening. How our inside world colors our perceptions!
They are never separate; for now, my ever deepening love of you
spills out of me and washes over everyone, over everything, the
five years of daily adoration of your Chinese face making everyone with similar features look beautiful to me. In some sense,
because of you, I feel that I belong here.

We duck into a tiny noodle shop and order chicken lo mein.
People stare at you here, too, just as they did earlier on the
street, but you act as if you don't notice, tossing your hair and
laughing as you twirl the slippery noodles on your fork, es-
chewing the chopsticks entirely. I look at you too, I can hardly
eat; something has happened to you, some light has turned on
in you since we arrived here. No longer a girl from nowhere in
your own mind . . . but now, a girl from China who has seen
China, heard China, and felt China. I know that soon it will be
time to tell you our story.

We step back into the street and get caught up in the river of
people; there are so many people here, Lily. I notice a sign in
Chinese and English that reads PHARMACY, and we step into the
dark cool interior. It is a long, narrow passage lined with shelves
from floor to ceiling. The shelves are packed with bottles, vials,
packages, and jars, all with some mysterious medicinal purpose. A Chinese man in a blue smock stands behind the
counter and grunts an acknowledgment as we walk in. You hold
my hand even more tightly and say, "Mommy, what do we need
in here?" You press against me, wanting assurance, wanting to

be shielded from the penetrating eyes of the man behind the counter.

"Some medicine for Daddy," I reply. He started feeling queasy this morning, and is waiting for us in the hotel room, resting from the long flight. I wonder if his being here, in China for the first time, is just too overwhelming.

I approach the man, and ask, "Do you speak English?"

He nods his head up and down emphatically. "What you need?" He stands and looks over the counter at us, squinting; first at me, then down at you, then back at me. His face is blank but his eyes are lively; he looks back at you again and holds his gaze there for a long moment. I begin to tell him, "My husband is feeling nauseous." I put my hand on my abdomen and grimace. "Stomach."

The man looks back at me, says, "Aha!" and reaches around me to retrieve something from one of the shelves. He plucks a small vial from the shelf and says, "This, good! Stomach!" as he hands the vial to me. I look at the vial; the label is written entirely in Chinese and there is a picture of some kind of plant on the front.

I hand the man some dollar bills and he takes them. But all the time, his eyes never leave you. We turn to go, and finally he says, "This . . . your daughter?" pointing to you, a quizzical, shy look on his face.

"Yes," I say. "She is my daughter. We live in the United States."

The man nods slowly. "She, beautiful," he says.

"Yes," I say, feeling a flutter inside, suddenly wanting to cry. I was afraid of what he was going to say, half expected some type of admonishment or inquiry about why we were together. For an instant I had wondered if it might be best not to tell him the truth.

"She go to America, she become beautiful. She stay in China, she be *nothing!*" he says, with a definitive movement of his hand, slicing the air with his flat open palm.

She be nothing, he said. My mind reels. How can a child, a girl, no matter where she is, be nothing? I mumble something as you pull me from the little store. We don't speak as we walk the few blocks back to the hotel, we are both tired now. The jumble of Chinese signs, the smell of sizzling food, the chattering of thousands of voices, create a perceptual bubble that surrounds us like the humid air of this city.

When we get to our room, Daddy is sleeping soundly and we try not to disturb him as I bathe you and help you get dressed for bed. I tuck you in with your blanket and a kiss. Before you close your eyes, you look at me intently, and ask, "Mommy, when we get the baby tomorrow, do we get to keep her? Forever?"

"Yes, Lily," I say. "Forever. She will be with us forever." You smile and settle into the pillows, and before long you are asleep. Two years ago when you started asking for a sister, I thought it was a passing phase, but you persisted, begged, and cajoled for an entire year. "*Please* can we go to China and get a baby?" you would plead. For you then, the only way a baby could possibly come into this world was through China.

By the time you started asking, I had already begun having dreams of another little girl who was waiting, who was longing for us. When your Daddy and I finally agreed that yes, it was time to go back to China and bring that baby home, you were elated, and immediately started planning for her arrival.

"We will need diapers, Mommy," you would say. "Can we please go to Target and get her a high chair?" You had a list in your head that rivaled mine; for I already knew that none of these things were really necessary. We had none of that for you, not even a diaper in the house when you arrived; all that was needed was love.

There is a stillness in the room, though the noise from the street and the whir of the air conditioner intrude upon the silence. I know that tonight I will not sleep. Too many memories are surfacing, too many thoughts about you, about the daughter I will meet tomorrow, about fate and miracles. I picture how your face might look when you first see your new sister, the nine-month-old baby that is waiting for us right now in Guangzhou; another pearl ejected from the mouth of the mighty dragon, another treasure entrusted to us.

How could I not have known that what affects a tiny orphaned girl in China affects me too? And yet I had not known, not really known. These years have been spent uncovering truths long buried, mining the rich earth of dreams and clues given but not noticed before. Praying for guidance and receiving it, in abundance; refining my will so that my life can be a force for good.

And loving you. For six weeks after we returned, you could have been taken from us at any moment. Legally you were not our child, and I bathed you, fed you, rocked you to sleep, and held you close with the thought always hovering: this could be all the time we have together; we have only now. The sheer joy of being near you protected me from despair, and those first intense days of uncertainty were a crucible in which the final shreds of my old life were burned away.

One cold gray day two weeks after we returned from China, the day before Christmas Eve, Alex called and said she needed to come and see me, she needed to talk. As I hung up the phone, I knew that this was what I had been dreading, that somehow the time had come when I would have to make a stand.

When Alex arrived, she was visibly nervous, and she sat down at my kitchen table with hardly a glance at you, playing on the floor, happy and content. "I think I may have made a mistake," she said, and I thought, Here it comes: the denouement, the crisis point, the Waterloo of this lifetime epic. "Maybe I should take her home for a day or so, just so I can be sure?" Her tone was firm, but her words, the "maybe," the "so I can be sure," told me everything I needed to know about her true intent. Her tentativeness fanned my anger and gave me courage. I took a deep breath and rose to my full height in the chair, and something like righteous certainty permeated my mind.

"You can't do that," I said, loud and strong. "You will not take her from this house." You will never take her from me again.

Alex slumped in her chair, the nervous bravado gone. She instantly became like a shell of herself in the face of my declaration, and she said "I know" with such sheepishness that I almost felt sorry for her. It surprised me how easily she let it go, and as she began trying to explain herself and save face, I knew it was done. The final act of our drama had been played out, and the curtain fell, releasing us from our roles in each other's lives.

I walked her to the door, and as I stood in the cold and watched her go, I felt a cloak of calm descend upon me; my worst fear had been faced. I knew with certainty that nothing would ever separate me from you again, and that certainty allowed me to release all blame. I said a silent prayer of thanks to Alex that in the end, she had done the right thing; her actions had brought you into my life. From the deepest part of me came forgiveness, and I let her go.

The first year you were with us I cried almost every day, and so did you. I cried when I remembered the faces of the other babies, the ones left behind. You cried whenever I tried to put you down; you did not want us to be apart for even a second. Many days you woke screaming in terror, and you could not be consoled. I would cry with you until you stopped, and after a time, the terror subsided, and you trusted you were safe.

I spent much time wondering how this had all happened. In thinking back, I realized I had been seeing you with me for so long, in dreams or visualizations, that it was almost as if my longing brought you into being. For years I had seen myself holding the hand of a little girl, and walking on the beach. She is with me now, that girl I dreamed of; and as I watch you sleep, I can hardly believe this dream is real. Through the grace of you my life has blossomed.

When I returned from China, when my family met you, my sister asked me if I remembered the time I had spoken Chinese.

"What? I have no idea what you are talking about!" I said.

She was stunned that I did not remember. We had taken a family trip to San Francisco, the summer I was fifteen. I remembered walking around that fog-shrouded city; it had seemed like a dream. We had been to Chinatown one day, and apparently that night in the hotel room, I sat up in bed and began speaking. My sister told me that I was quite upset about something, and kept waving my arms around, saying something about a baby. I was crying, and then I lay back down and went to sleep. She said she was quite scared, and that she was sure I was speaking Chinese.

"How do you know?" I asked her.

She said it sounded exactly like what we had been hearing all day in Chinatown.

"That's why I wasn't surprised," she said.

"Weren't surprised about what?" I asked.

"About you bringing home the baby. I always knew you were Chinese."

A chill of recognition rippled over me as she spoke those words, and I thought, Yes, I am Chinese. Perhaps I have been every race, color, creed, and nationality in some lifetime that I do not recall, but that influences me still. Since bringing you home, whenever I see a Chinese or Asian face, a feeling of kinship, of connection and knowing, rises in me, to meet that person with the same eyes, the same hair, the same skin as my Lily. How could I not be one with them, when I love you so? I forget at times that when they look at me, they see someone different, someone separate; and when I remember that, it feels like a betrayal.

I want to say to them, do you not see? We are the same, underneath these superficial characteristics that make us look different to each other. I want to share with them what I know: that it is there for us to discover, the offspring of our deathless souls, in our dreams and desires, in the places that beckon us, in the people we long for, in the loves and fears with which we dance.

But I do not say it, I never do. I just hold you close, and hope that they see in our love a hopeful beacon calling them to life. Tomorrow we will hold another child in our arms, that love will be multiplied, and as I watch you sleep, I know that for you, I have been reborn.

Acknowledgments

I am grateful to many people who have been instrumental in bringing this book to life. First and foremost to my husband, Randy, who believed in this book and never wavered in his support. Thank you for the many years of encouragement, but most of all, thank you for saying yes and allowing the miracle of Lily into our lives.

To Paula Bansch, who deserves much of the credit for keeping me on track during so many phases of this book project, thank you for your enthusiasm, your excellent judgment on all matters literary, and your very good taste in wine. Thank you to Antoinette Carr for your guidance, wisdom, and love over the course of many years, and to Paige Ohliger, for friendship that went above and beyond the call of duty during the writing of this book.

Thank you to my agent, Liza Dawson, for taking a chance on this book and on me. Your expert advice and counsel is invaluable. To my editor at Touchstone/Fireside, Amanda Patten, thank you for the care, consideration, and patience you have shown throughout this process. You and your colleagues at Touchstone have been impressive in all that you have done, and I am sincerely grateful that I have had the chance to work with you.

Thank you to my family: my father, Paul Nonte, my brothers, Bill and Paul, and my sisters Cathy and Barbie, and my late sister, Patrice, who passed away earlier this year. Your love and support mean the world to me, and it has been fun sharing in the excitement of this book with you.

And last but not least, to my daughters, Lily and Jaden: you inspire me each and every day. Thank you for bringing your love and light into my life.

GOLDEN PHOENIX
FOUNDATION
DEDICATED TO THOSE LEFT BEHIND

The Golden Phoenix Foundation was established in 2006 in order to assist in improving the quality of life of orphans around the world. For more information about our work in helping those left behind, please visit our website: www.golden phoenixfoundation.org.

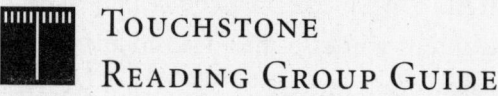

Forever Lily

Discussion Questions

1. What does the author reveal about her personal life and character in the first chapter by telling her story in the first person? What do we know about her that she does not tell us explicitly? Why do you think the author chose to use the present tense to tell this story?

2. Considering they weren't the closest of friends, why do you think Beth agreed to accompany Alex to China? Why do you think Alex asked Beth to come with her to China?

3. When the adoption agency brings the baby to Alex, she is markedly disappointed. What is your opinion of Alex at this moment? What are your feelings toward Alex by the end of the book?

4. What would you do if you were an adoptive mother and you did not bond with your prospective child? If the author had

not accompanied Alex to China, what do you think would have happened to the baby?

5. Do you think the author was destined to go to China and adopt Lily? If what happened was destiny, and events were meant to unfold as they did, how does this affect your feelings about Alex? What role does choice play in destiny?

6. When the author confesses her need to adopt Lily to her husband, are you surprised by his response? What does this tell you about their relationship? How would such a situation have been handled in your own marriage or primary relationship?

7. How do the author's dreams relate to what is happening during her waking hours? What do the dreams add to the telling of the story? Have you personally experienced significant dreams that have had an impact on your life?

8. In the prologue to *Forever Lily*, Russell writes, "Dying is nothing like we suppose." Is the author talking about death literally or metaphorically? When looking at the dream sequences in *Forever Lily*, what does death symbolize to the author?

9. After reading *Forever Lily*, what are your impressions of China? Did they change as a result of reading this? Compare how women are viewed in the United States as opposed to how they are viewed in China.

10. In *Forever Lily*, spiritual thought and prayer play a major role in how the author processes her experience. Do you think the outcome would have been the same had this not been the case? Why or why not?

Interview with Beth Nonte Russell

1. *Since you were not a working writer at the time you went to China, how did you come to the decision to write* Forever Lily, *and why?*

Though I had never written for publication, writing was something I enjoyed and did regularly before this trip took place. When I returned from China, I knew beyond a doubt that I would write this story and try to share it with others. It felt quite different in that there was a strong urge to tell others about the abandoned children that I had seen in the orphanage there; I felt obligated to be their voice. Thoughts of those children would not let me go, and I began writing the book a year after I returned. One night, I finally sat down and wrote the passages that describe the orphanage visit, and that section, those images, became the heart of the book.

2. *Now that time has passed and you have perspective on what happened during your first trip to China, why do you think Alex asked you to accompany her?*

I believe that she was prompted to do so by an unconscious need to balance the karma between us. As the experience in China proved to me, there is always much more at work in any given situation than we are aware of on a conscious level, and in the case of Alex and my friendship, I believe the "much more" that was at work was a karmic debt from a past lifetime in which she was instrumental in my having lost a child. In this lifetime, she was given the opportunity to balance that debt by asking me to accompany her to China, and I was given the opportunity to accept a gift of love into my life.

3. *What is your relationship with Alex and her family today?*

My husband and Alex's husband made an agreement that following the adoption hearing we would have no further contact between our families. We all agreed this was best for everyone concerned, especially Lily, and we have never regretted that decision.

4. *What were the biggest differences between your experiences with mothering your stepchildren and your adoptive children? What were the biggest factors that contributed to these differences?*

In the case of my stepchildren, they already had a mother whom they loved and who loved them. I played a parental role, but not a central role, in their lives. I was not their mother, and therefore the emotional connection was of a different nature, perhaps less intense. I don't consider Lily and Jaden my "adoptive" children; they are just my children in the most complete sense. Their father and I have total responsibility for their welfare, and I doubt they think of me as their "adoptive" mother. . . . I am their mother with no qualifiers attached to that term.

5. *The dream sequences are quite detailed and follow a distinct narrative path. Were they changed or embellished for the telling of* Forever Lily?

The dreams as I experienced them in China were less complete and more fractured than the way I recount them in the book. When I returned from China, I spent many hours in meditation, reentering the dreams, which were actually a past-life experience. In that way, I was able to gain access to the narrative of that lifetime as well as minute and colorful details. In writing the book, I combined actual dreams with details, which I found out later through those meditations, in order to give the reader a sense that the dreams were indicating a complete lifetime.

6. *Memoir is one of the most risky literary forms because one person's "truth" can be quite a bit different from another person's "truth," which can have profound consequences on relationships. How did you decide which aspects of your life to include in* Forever Lily?

The experience of reality is always subjective. With *Forever Lily,* I did not set out to write a memoir, to tell "about" my life; instead, I hoped to give the reader a chance to share the experience and bridge the gap of subjectivity. My primary intention was to let the reader enter my internal psychological, emotional, and spiritual process as it took place in the context of this particular event. And also, I hoped to show that the transformation which occurred for me during this trip was not random or sudden; the forces of that transformation had been building for many years. For that reason, I included only those things from my life which I felt would be helpful in understanding how and why this happened the way that it did, hoping that perhaps it would give others a road map for their own transformational process.

7. *In the five years between your visits, China had changed dramatically. When you adopted your second daughter, what were the biggest differences in the process?*

The two trips were dramatically different, but not so much because of the five-year interval or the changes within China. They were different because the second adoption was intentional on our part, and we were able to prepare emotionally in a way that was not possible in the first adoption. Another big difference was that our girls came from different regions of a vast country. During the first trip, we traveled to very poor, rural areas in central China, which was grueling; in the second, we stayed in the large and thriving southern city of Guangzhou with all the amenities that city had to offer. My sense was that the process of adoption had not changed much, if at all, in the five-year span between trips.

8. *Why was Josephine worried for you while you were in China?*
   The answer to that question is actually very complicated. Though Josephine is not psychic, she is gifted in being able to discern certain things in the metaphysical realm which are outside most people's awareness. In her view, something of immense importance was taking place while I was in China, and her concern was that something would happen to prevent it from unfolding. She was concerned for both my spiritual and my physical safety, mainly because the lifetime which this event was resolving had ended in my premature physical death in ancient China. Events have a tendency to repeat themselves until the cycles are broken, and my bringing this baby home safely was a breakthrough in that regard, for me as well as for the many others involved in both lifetimes, including Josephine herself.

9. *How did Josephine react to your decision to adopt a second baby? Is she still your spiritual advisor?*
   Josephine's goal as a spiritual advisor is to help the client understand and utilize his or her own power, which is always within. My original agreement with her was to work together

for three years, and when that time was up, we continued to speak often, though our work together became more of a partnership. She gave advice and counsel based on her understandings, but in the end, it was always up to me to decide the best course of action. When I first told her I was going to China, she advised me not to go, and when I told her of my plans to adopt a second child, in her opinion, it was not a good idea. But once the decisions were made, whether I took her advice or not, she could help me to make the most of the situation by utilizing prayer and helping me to understand the situation in a much deeper way.

10. *What is your favorite aspect of the Chinese culture? How do you share these customs with your children?*

Though I have grown to love many things about China, I am not an expert on Chinese culture. There is so much focus on these girls being Chinese, but in my view, I am raising two American daughters who happen to have been born in China. They spent the earliest few months of their lives there and will spend the great majority of their lives here, but I do hope that at some point they will have an interest in the land of their birth. To that end, I have begun a library of books about China for my daughters to read when they are ready, and I also hope to travel with them to China many times in the coming years. Because Chinese history is complicated, especially where the circumstances of their lives are concerned, it is important to be very thoughtful in the way Chinese culture is discussed with them. My hope is that my girls will gain a deeper understanding of China over time and be able to make their own decisions about how far they want to take that interest.

Activities

1. Invite parents who have adopted a child from another country to your reading group to share the challenges they faced, from the initial decision-making process, to how they dealt with the confusing paperwork, to traveling to their child's country of origin, to life in the United States afterward.

2. Set the mood for your *Forever Lily* reading group meeting by playing Chinese music and serving Chinese food. The author recommends "Silk Road Journeys," by the cellist Yo Yo Ma, and music from the Beijing Angelic Children's Choir, both of which she used while writing *Forever Lily*.

3. Research the symbols that are most prevalent in *Forever Lily* and discuss their meaning in Chinese and esoteric mythology. For example: the dragon, the lotus, shoes, the dove, the kite, etc.

4. Discuss personal experiences of your own that may have been outside the norm, such as strange dreams or visions, and explore the ways in which they made an impact on your life or a decision-making process.